LONG TO REIGN OVER US . . .

LONG TO REIGN OVER US . . .

*Memories of Coronation Day
and of life in the 1950s*

EDITED BY
KENNETH and VALERIE McLEISH

BLOOMSBURY

This edition published in 1992
by Bloomsbury Publishing Limited
2 Soho Square, London W1V 5DE

The moral rights of the authors have been asserted.

Individual memories copyright © the letter-writers
Arrangement and editorial comment © 1992 Kenneth and Valerie McLeish.
Design copyright © 1992 Bloomsbury Publishing Limited.

Illustrations
1, 9, 10 11 © Camera Press Ltd; 2, 3 © *Daily Mail*/Solo; 4, 7, 8 © Popperfoto; 5 © *Daily Mail*; 12, 13, 14, 15, 16 with kind permission of, respectively, Frederick Walkden, Pamela Heath, Bernard Polley, Marion Olley, Maxine Bonner

Map of the Coronation procession on pp vi–vii reproduced with kind permission of the The Royal Jubilee Trusts

A copy of the CIP entry of this book is avilable from the British Library.

ISBN 0 7475 1267 1

10 9 8 7 6 5 4 3 2 1

Designed by Geoff Green
Typeset by Hewer Text Composition Services, Edinburgh
Printed by Clays Ltd. St Ives plc, Bungay, Suffolk

The editors would like to thank Jane Reddin, who word-processed all the letters, and Nicky Thompson, who copy-edited the final manuscript.

CONTENTS

Introduction		ix
Contributors		xi

THE WAY WE WERE

1	Hard Times	3
2	An Englishman's Home . . .	10
3	Country Life	19
4	Food	26
5	Shops	36
6	Children	43
7	The Festival of Britain	59
8	Floods	61
9	Work	70
10	What Times We Had!	82
11	Getting About	94
12	Death of George VI	98
13	Everest	103

GOD SAVE THE QUEEN

14	Getting Ready	109
15	Take Your Places, Please	118
16	In the Abbey	135
17	Vivat, Vivat Regina!	144
18	'Looking In'	151
19	Celebrating	163
20	Coronation Day	173
21	Coronation Postscript	185

LOOKING BACK ON THE 1950s

| 22 | What Were Those Days *Really* Like? | 193 |

CORONATION
OF HER MAJEST

OFFICIAL
ROUTE

ROCESSION
QUEEN ELIZABETH II

INTRODUCTION

Queen Elizabeth II was crowned on Tuesday 2 June 1953. It rained. So history books tell us, in their brisk, efficient way. They usually go on to provide lists of who was there, what was said and done, and what happened afterwards.

It is all true, all important – but unless you are a historian, all potentially boring. Most history books are concerned mainly with 'important' people and 'great' events. They rarely describe what was happening in the everyday lives of ordinary people. And for most 'ordinary' Britons at the time, the Coronation was one of the most exciting, most colourful events in their entire lives. People still remember it as vividly as if it happened yesterday – and can tell you exactly what they were doing, what they were thinking, as the processions and other historic events took place.

Such 'ordinary' memories are what inspired this book. We wanted to hear what people remembered, what they were doing and thinking on 2 June 1953. But there was more. The Coronation was not an isolated event. Its importance came partly from its surroundings: the life and time of the early 1950s. We thought that any book about it should include memories of what life was like: we wanted to ask people, 'What did you do, how did you manage, forty years ago?'

This book is a tapestry of memories. We advertised in local newspapers, clubs and libraries, asking people to write to us about what they remembered about Coronation Day and the events surrounding it – and about their lives in the 1950s generally. We had hundreds of replies, some short, others running to a dozen pages or more. People sent photographs, newspaper cuttings, magazines and books. Single anecdotes, long descriptions, even a couple of short stories – all gave glimpses of what seemed important or interesting to 'ordinary' individuals at the time.

We would like to thank everyone who took the trouble to write to us. Their letters kick-started our own recollections of the 1950s. We'd like to dedicate this book to everyone whose memory, like ours, is a ragbag – and to anyone who remembers such things as putting nail varnish on stockings to stop them laddering . . . collecting string . . . sealing wax . . . wearing white gloves in summer . . . sports jackets and duffel coats . . . listening to *Children's Hour* . . . watching Muffin the Mule . . . cheering as Roger Bannister ran the first four-minute mile . . . reading about Laika, the first dog in space . . . mending broken suspenders with aspirin tablets . . . ration books . . . Alma Cogan . . . crêpe-soled shoes . . .

Kenneth and Valerie McLeish
Spalding 1992

CONTRIBUTORS

Mavis Abraham, R.J. Allen, Barbara Allman, Phoebe Ames, Jacky Armstrong, Mrs J. Ashenden, Lottie Ashenden, Harry Ashford, Lynne Atkinson, Alan Baker, Richard Balfe, Arnold Bamfrith, Gillian Bark, Jeannie Barnes, Pamela Barnett, Rita Beckett, 'Su' Bentham, Audrey Berry, Olive Beveridge, Leslie Blowers, Pamela Bowen, Arthur Brand, Joyce Brandreth, Rena Brewin, Jo Brodie, Elisabeth Brooke, Barbara Browne, P. Bryant, Catherine Burns, Marion Bunting, Donald Burling, John Marris Burwood, Olive Butcher, Genie Carson, Bob Clarke, Catharine D. Clarke, Harry Coles, Ronald Coley, Barbara Coley-Donohue, Ellen Cooke, The Coombes Croft Library Local History Group, Philomena Cooper, P.E. Corbett, Marie Couldwell, Colin Coupland, Susan Cran, Jane Fraser Cross, Joan Cutner, Ruth Daly, Elsie Darby, William Davies BEM, Mrs G. Dix, David Dixon, Irene Dowie, R.A. Dowling, Patricia and Peter Elcoate, Maxine Elvey, Robert O. Erricker, Jane Fabb, Anne Filkin, Sheila Francis, Pat Freestone, Eileen Fry, Geoffrey Gardner, Brian Garner, V.E. Glazebrook, Frank Goldsworthy, Jean Gostelow, V. Gray, Hazel Green, Norman Green, J.A. Grimes, Mr E.H., Bob Hallowell, Molly Hames, Mrs F.E. Hamill, Pat Harker, Joan Harper, Val Hastings, Mrs J.K. Hawkins, Gwen Heath, Valerie Heath, Charles Heriot, Sylvia Hulme, Suzanne Hulott, Captain E. W. Jackson OBE, Dorothy A. Jacques of Nottingham, Margaret Jarrett, Janet Johnston, Rachel Jones, Mrs Haydée A. Kent, Mrs Leonie Kitchener, Doreen Knox, Harry Lawson, Eve Lecomber, Mrs Dorothy Ludlow, Muriel McDermott, Mrs D.J. McDonald, Stella McLeish, Harold Mack, Margaret Mackie, Doris Matthews, Sherrie Meigs, Marjorie Miller, Pat Miller, Rosemary Miller, Harry Molyneux-Seel-Unsworth, Joan Moor, Sylvia Moore, Isobel Mordy, Sheila McGregor Morgan, Geoffrey Morris, Gina Murphy, Madge Nicol, Doris Nicholson, Diane A.

Noble, Eric Norris (Master Bookseller), Marion Olley, Robin Ollington, Howard Palmer, Cedric Parcell, Mrs B.S. Payne, Grace Peary, Gwendolen Piggott, Margaret Pollard, Bernard Polley, Ellen Poole, Joan Poole, Peter Poole, Kath Price, Irene Pugh, Harry Reeve, Phyllis Reeve, Rosemary Ridyard, Peggy Close Riedtmann, Evelyn D. Riegert, Ian Roberts, Margaret Robinson, Margaret A. Rodgers, Mrs E.M.G. Rogers, Dorothy Royston, Ernie Rumsey, Peter Ryde, Pat Salmon, Mrs A. Saville, Molly Schuessele, Geoffrey W. Shardlow, Peter Simmonds, H. B. Smith, John C. Smith, Phyllis Smith, Wendy Smith, Mrs A. Southon, Colin Stephens, Daphne Stone, Bryan Taylor, Keith Taylor, Patricia Thomas, Mrs C.S. Thornton, Kenneth Townsend, John Tyrrell, Mary Underhay, Frederick Walkden, Pat Warnes, Irene Watson, Muriel Weaver, Phyllis Webb, Maureen Weitman, Mrs West, Rose Whittle, Peter Wickings, Carol Williams, Ms Kay Wilson, Pat Wilson, Sheila Wilson, John Wilton, Mary Winstone, Rhoda Woodward, Mrs B.M. Woulds, Maria Wrist.

THE WAY WE WERE

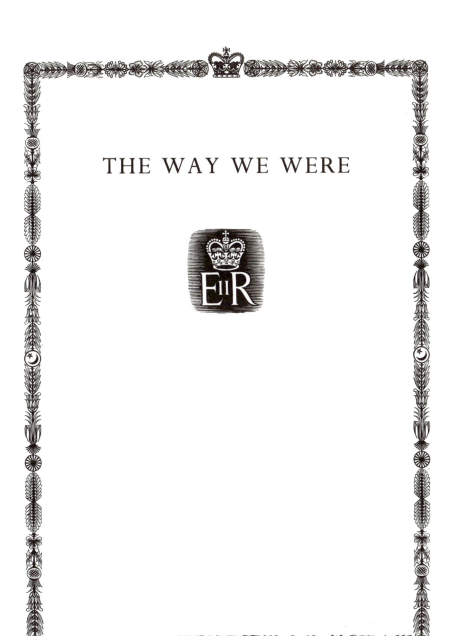

1

HARD TIMES

For us, happiness was three sardines on a slice of toast.
                                                    Ronald Coley

If you ask people what life was like forty years ago, their memories are complicated by the fact that they were so much younger then (and sometimes healthier and happier) than they are today. Often, they think of the past as freer, more cheerful and certainly more honest than life in the 1990s.

This is true of some of the people who wrote to us about the 1950s – and it applies to some of our own memories, too. But a second theme also runs through many of the letters: that existence in Britain, during the Second World War and the years of austerity which followed, had been pared to the bone. Most people managed, but life was often poor, hard and comfortless. Ronald Coley writes, with feeling:

Above all else, my abiding memory of the 1950s is that of the cold. Cold houses, cold trains, cold cinemas and theatres; waking up to a freezing house and having to come downstairs, rake the ashes, relight the fire and pray there would be enough fuel to do the same the next day and the day after that.

Two entries from Ruth Daly's 1954 diary tell their own chilly story:

Wednesday 6 January: It was very cold and wet today. The water at school froze on Tuesday night, and the taps were turned on but not off before we went home. Water came through the ceiling into the girls' cloakroom, so the girls had to wear their coats all day.

Thursday 7 January: It was very cold today. I wore three pairs of socks and two pairs of gloves, and I was still freezing. The girls had to wear their coats in school again, because the ceiling was still dripping with water. I played netball in the afternoon with my gloves, blazer and hat on because it was so cold.

3

Another problem, far commoner then than now, was air pollution. In the days of coal fires – thousands upon thousands of coal fires – whole cities were regularly smothered in choking 'smog' (a mixture of smoke and fog). John Tyrrell remembers setting off to cycle into Bradford one March day, and being caught halfway there in a smog so dense that it was like being wrapped in a blanket. It was impossible for him to see the kerb at his feet or the handlebars of the bike he was pushing. In the winter of 1952 John Marris Burwood and his wife, flying to England from South Africa, had to stop over in Kenya, where they were told that their journey

. . . would be delayed indefinitely because London was blacked out by a massive smog consisting of heavy layers of ash covering all the rooftops. Many cattle were killed in Smithfield market, and many old people died.

Harold Mack comments:
These fogs had to be experienced to be believed. One January night in 1951, when I left work, darkness had already set in. With my bicycle I crossed the river through the foot tunnel under the Thames, because no ferry was operating. It was impossible to ride the bike because I couldn't see the road. I walked the four miles home. I remember finding it quite difficult to breathe in the swirling yellow smog. Late that night my brother-in-law arrived on his bicycle (the fog must have thinned) to inform us that my Dad had phoned my sister to say that Mum had died that evening. She'd been ill for months, but that fog had robbed her of enough breath to live. The funeral had to be postponed for ten days because so many people who had died in that particular suffocating fog had to be buried or cremated.

Harold Mack remembers another kind of pollution, common in cities during the 1950s – and long-standing, in London at least, since people complained of it in Dickens' and Shakespeare's times:
One of the differences between then and now was the pollution in the rivers. The water would be black, and I have seen dead cats and dogs floating down with the current. Believe it or not, on one occasion, in that same river there was a dead horse. Sometimes in hot summer weather, when the ferry paddle wheels were in action, the smell was enough to make one gag.

On the banks of city rivers in the 1950s, and in the roads and streets, tattiness often prevailed. Until well into the decade, there seemed to be no spare cash, no spare energy or willpower, to clear up the mess left by wartime bombing. John Tyrrell recalls heaps of rubble so weathered over the years that they had turned to gritty sand. Mrs A. Saville writes of colonies of feral cats, offspring of once-cherished pets made homeless by bombing. Susan Cran says that the dereliction and drabness of the streets made her feel uneasy at the time (she was a young child), and now seem to sum up the mood of the early 1950s. Maxine Elvey remembers

. . . naked walls with their wallpaper hanging, and marks of where stairs and floors had been, but above all black, spiral fire escapes, which were sometimes all that remained of a building and hung in the middle of nowhere.

Small wonder, when things were as bleak as this, that many people took the chance to escape. Throughout the 1950s, emigration was common. Sherrie Meigs says that although she 'felt like a rat leaving a sinking ship', she could 'no longer put up with the bleakness and the greyness' and knew that she 'simply had to get away'. Harold Mack, like many emigrants, was astounded at the quality, and energy, of life away from Britain:

Two things sum up these impressions. After I went to Canada, I first worked at the live-on-the-job construction of a paper mill, and the first morning the breakfast was bacon and egg for several hundred hungry men. During the war, when I was in the RAF, to provide bacon and eggs for breakfast had meant that the cooks started cooking two hours before, and kept it hot in the ovens for an hour or so. RAF breakfast eggs were like rubber, and bacon was crisp as a biscuit. At Canada Construction, the cooks had eggs and bacon cooking on a giant hotplate and served them as fresh and as hot as at home.

The other surprise in Canada was when my family arrived. The construction job had finished and I had to get another job. One couldn't get a job without a telephone, as prospective employers would take your application but without a phone number wouldn't bother to contact you. If a firm in Canada want to employ you, they need you 'now'. We were renting a house at this time, and I went to the telephone company to apply for a home phone. Being familiar with the London system, with a wait of about six months, I was surprised, to say the least, when the girl looked at my application and said, 'I'm sorry, Mr Mack, but we won't be able to install your phone – until this afternoon'!

Barbara Coley-Donohue sheds more light on Canadian attitudes to their immigrants – and by implication, on the way some immigrants must have behaved:
You didn't dare say anything was better 'at home', or you were told, 'There are two ships leaving daily'. One day at work, I hadn't opened my mouth when I was told, 'I suppose you're going to tell us how you did it at home?'

In another part of the world, equally far away, Britons were having a much tougher time. Most soldiers in battle feel neglected, or forgotten, by the people back home. But Britons who fought for the UN forces supporting South Korea in the Korean War (1950–53) had more reason than most to be bitter. At home, people had other things on their minds: national recovery and rationing, to name just two. None the less, for young national servicemen sent to Korea, and for their families waiting anxiously for news, the war was real enough. Kenneth Townsend writes of one horrific battle, on 22 April 1951, in which, out of 750 men from his regiment (the Gloucesters) only forty-six survived. At about the same time Robert O. Erricker and the rest of his tank-crew were captured by the North Koreans. He remembers the grim trek north to a POW camp:
We marched at night, in a straight line over the paddies parallel to the 'road' (a track, in our view). The snow clung to the heels of our boots and, having to kick it off every few steps, made each pace more agonizing and slower. One just kept going, on and on, and continuously in our minds were the questions, 'Where are we going, and what will happen to us?'

Thank goodness for the British tank suit. All zipped up, hood up, head down, hands in pockets, one just followed the figure in front. We were not allowed to stop to relieve ourselves: if we did it was 'Huba, huba' and a gesture with a rifle. Some nights we'd march/ walk all night, others for just three or four hours. We soon learned to dry our boots during the day, as they got very sweaty walking in wet snow. We dried them as we slept, as we had to take them off before going into the Korean houses.

It was not until some two months after Coronation Day that the war ended and the prisoners were repatriated. Robert Erricker writes:
On 9 August 1953, after early breakfast at 07.00, we got into the truck for the journey to Panmunjom. Along the road we passed countless items of American equipment discarded by released Chinese

and North Korean ex-POWs: their way of showing their displeasure at the American system. There were about twenty of us, and at 09.00 hours exactly we crossed over to freedom and Britannia Camp, where we filed into a marquee. The first job was to be deloused: arms outstretched, a yank on either side, DDT up our sleeves and another lot down our trousers.

We travelled by boat up the Inland Sea from Osaka to Kure, where the boys who'd been released earlier were waiting for us. We were shown our barracks and all our kit laid out. I was a veteran at not quite twenty-two! After documentation and medicals, we were free to visit Hiro and Kure and to shop for souvenirs. If you bought a metal suitcase, the Japanese painted your name and address free of charge, and there were dozens of these suitcases going home on the *Asturias*.

Korea is indelibly printed on my mind, and not a day or a week goes by without my remembering some aspect of it. I remember the boys who fell in Happy Valley. I remember Sergeant Ted Collins, recalled from the reserve, who left a beautiful wife and two young children. I remember the young ones killed in action, whose parents were to receive the dreaded knock at the door by the telegram-boy. I remember the boys who died in the POW camp, for whom we could do nothing. I remember the unwashed, unshaven, lice-ridden, stinking bodies on the long march, the starvation and the dysentery (the biggest killer of all). Above all, I remember absent friends.

Back home, people knew little of such horrors, halfway across the world. But though our struggle was less lethal, it was just as grim. Jean Gostelow writes:
I can't imagine why anyone looks back with pleasure at the 1950s. We'd been through so much already – the First World War, the Depression, the Second World War – and now we just felt flattened. We thought we'd earned a rest, a little bit of comfort – and all we had was the unending grind of trying to make ends meet. People say 'Our lives were so much simpler then'. Of course they were! We had so little that whenever a little bit of cheer came our way – a warm snap in winter, a bright new song on the wireless, a night out with a friend, even just a box of that rarity in those days, chocolates – we felt as though we'd been given the sun, moon and stars. We were fed up with greyness; we were ready for a little glamour. The only problem was, neither we nor our leaders seemed to have the least idea how we were to get it.

Maxine Elvey adds:

If I think of the 1950s, I think of drabness. Even as children, my sister and I were conscious of living in a drab world. Most clothes were drab in colour: beige, moss green, etc. I remember when we were small, five or six, my aunt made us dresses for a wedding, of a lovely pale blue cotton voile, with smocking on the bodices which must have taken her hours to do. I remember the lovely blue like a spring sky, it made such a contrast with our other clothes.

Drabness ruled in other ways. Books and magazines were less colourful, because colour printing was so much less sophisticated. Children's books had mostly line drawings, with a few 'colour plates' on a different kind of paper, often glossy, printed on one side and inserted. Newspapers had no colour pages or colour supplements. There were few colour photos in magazines. People took black-and-white photos, and TV and most films were in black and white.

In 1990 I visited Pula in Yugoslavia. It was a run-down, decaying town, with hardly any shops. Those which did exist sold a limited range of goods. I would imagine that most post-Communist countries nowadays still have the air we remember in western Europe from just after the war. Certainly Britain was just like that.

It would be wrong, even so, to give the impression that life was nothing but gloom and drabness. Several people who wrote to us describe the 1950s much more cheerfully, talking about the simple things of life – the kind of ordinary, everyday things 'our boys' were fighting to preserve for the people of Korea. Two letters, from Rena Brewin and Rosemary Ridyard, offer a series of snapshots of British life in the 1950s, with good and bad mixed together. Rena Brewin writes:

I remember playing happily in the road – there was very little traffic – ball games, Cowboys and Indians, catch, hopscotch, etc. I remember listening to the wireless (a big wooden box in the corner), and being very quiet at Saturday tea time so that Dad could check his pools.

Every spring, my Gran put her fur coat in storage. A van used to bring a big cardboard box for it, and would take it away and bring it back in the autumn.

We had no heating upstairs in bedrooms or bathroom. We bathed once a week: more than that was extravagant. In the winter we all washed in the kitchen where it was warmer – except me: I would be washed in front of the living-room fire from a bowl on a stool.

I remember going down the allotment with Dad and helping him weed. I remember onions spread out all over the lawn to dry before they were pickled.

Rosemary Ridyard adds:
I don't think there was much in the way of help, moneywise, in those days before social security as we know it today. We always seemed to be hard up and had to scheme and save for such things as house decoration and holidays. There were no expensive toys for children in the working and middle classes, and people didn't buy each other expensive presents at Christmas and birthdays – they just weren't expected. In fact, it was still quite acceptable to make presents if possible.

There wasn't the money spent on weddings that there is today, nor were there any evening 'do's'. When the couple went away after the reception, that was it – unless family and close friends went back to view the wedding presents – and nobody had to guard the house when everyone was out, either. Marriages were normally for life then. Unmarried mothers were still a disgrace, and living together before marriage was unheard-of.

One thing about cars. When you acquired one, if you didn't have a garage you rented one. Cars just weren't left on the roadside as today.

Mrs A. Saville and Sylvia Hulme comment favourably on the behaviour of the time. Mrs Saville writes:
One good thing about those days: old-fashioned integrity and morality were still about. The crime wave had not yet started, and going out at night was safe, for both young and old. What's the use of having more money if you have to endure 'house arrest' and stay in every night?

Sylvia Hulme says:
Young men were expected to rise when ladies entered the room, offer seats on buses, open doors, assist with heavy books or bags, and be polite to their seniors.

And Margaret Jarrett, reflecting on the difference between then and now, echoes the feeling of the vast majority of people who wrote to us:
In those days life seemed much freer and more casual. I suppose there were snags – one only remembers the best things – but I'm glad I was young then and not now.

2

AN ENGLISHMAN'S HOME . . .

. . . is his castle.
Proverb

In fact, anyone who owned a castle in the 1950s was one of the lucky ones. Immediately after the war, there was a huge housing problem all over Britain. Houses were old and dilapidated after years of wartime neglect. Most towns and cities were cratered and scarred by bombs. There was little money to spare for renovation. In a few areas, where there was really desperate need, councils put up supposedly temporary 'prefabs'. These were two-room bungalows, little bigger than caravans – but still, as Harold Mack remembers, a great improvement on the alternative:

After about four years of living in other people's houses, in early 1948, with the birth of a second child, we were allotted a rented, brand-new council house at Wynford Bay, Mottingham. We now had our own castle: a concrete-construction house partly built by German POW labourers.

Other families were given houses on former wartime property, as Wendy Smith recalls:

June 1953 found our family living in mediocre accommodation in North Wales. To be more precise, it was an isolated bungalow, formerly an RAF officer's home, on a redundant airfield four miles from Caernarvon. At rising fourteen, and unsophisticated, I thought it and the surroundings wonderful. It had solid parquet floors painted shiny brown (no fitted carpets in those days), with loose rugs here and there and light wood utility furniture in abundance. There were concrete and metal surrounds on window-fittings, and the walls inside were finished with a raised swirly or spiky effect which scratched the unwary passer-by. The outside consisted of a portion of garden surrounded by fields, a brook, trees and scrub. Outhouses (formerly officers' messes etc.) accommodated pigs and hens, my enterprising father having set up a smallholding to eke out our meagre living.

But prefabs and ex-war-office properties were the exception. There was little new building, and in some places bomb-wrecked houses remained untouched for years. Building a million new homes was one of the pledges which helped to get the Conservative government elected in 1951 – and it was several more years before that promise could be fulfilled. In the meantime, people made do as best they could. Mr and Mrs W.G. Harper had no money to buy a house, even if one had been available. So, Joan Harper continues:
. . . we were delighted when my husband was offered a railway cottage (a tied house: he worked for the London, Midland and Scottish Railway Company), despite the fact that it had no running water, no gas, no electricity and no sanitation.

Compared to one London police constable and his wife, the Harpers were lucky. Forty years later, this young couple's early married life sounds like something from a TV sitcom, but it was no joke at the time:
In August 1953 we married and left for Torquay on the 'Honeymoon Express' as it was called, complete with ration books. On the return journey we counted our money, and all we had to our names was £5. We didn't have a place to live together at the time. I lived with my husband's mother, and he lived at the Police Section House just off Edgware Road. Although we were married, I wasn't allowed to go to his room, and our goodnights were said in shop doorways before I caught the train home to Sidcup.

These were the kind of problems which, in the late 1940s and early 1950s, inspired a major government scheme, designed to provide new housing on a massive scale. This was the new towns movement. The idea was to build new towns (on what are nowadays known as 'greenfield' sites, that is in the country), and to move people there from overcrowded or derelict city areas. Between 1946 and 1950, fourteen new towns were planned, each with a projected population of 25,000– 60,000. Planning was one thing, but building the towns and moving the people was a very different matter. Even in 1957, when Irene Pugh and her husband moved to Harlow New Town, what they found was hardly the idyll claimed by the original planners:

Rents averaged between £2–£3 per week; this included rates. We all seemed to be living on a shoe-string. Coming from London, where buses used to run so frequently, we were now really in the sticks. There was plenty of mud where roads had not been completed. No bus services. A country train service: the train unloaded the first half of passengers, then shunted forward to allow the passengers from the rear end of the train to alight. It was a long trek to the nearest welfare clinic. And of course there were the 'new town blues': many of us were lonely and missed our families.

As there was no employment of any kind in Harlow itself, my husband had only been offered the house if he continued to work in central London. His journey to the City took two hours or more each way by train, plus the walk to and from the station. Roads were narrow, there were no parking facilities for private vehicles, and there were very few garages for rent. The planners had not foreseen that the car would come into its own and become a way of life.

For people who preferred to stay where they were, life could be just as inconvenient – as Gillian Bark recalls:
We had to share a council house in a rough area with an old man who had previously had the house to himself. He didn't like girls, so didn't like me; but he doted on my brother. I used to be ill a lot: looking back, it may have been psychological, with him disliking me and the school and area being so rough. Eventually he died and the house was made over to my parents; then, because they were good tenants, we were given a new council house on the other side of town.

Such conditions inevitably caused stress and strain. Muriel McDermott remembers:
A lot of couples split up as they could not get a home. My first husband left me with two young children. I eventually remarried, and had my other three children, but thanks to the war it was hard to get a decent job and impossible to save.

Other people moved in with older relatives. Elsie Darby says that it was a good job her parents' house was a big one, as it had to accommodate her parents, her sister, brother-in-law and their two children, her husband and herself. Such sharing often worked well. Jane Fraser Cross remembers living with her parents in 1953, paying 25/- (£1.25) a week rent (out of a wage of £3-15s-11d, £3.80) – and says that it was one of the happiest years of her life. Maxine Elvey remembers her uncle, his

*wife and their baby son living upstairs in her grandmother's house for
'several years', and everyone accepting the arrangement very happily.
But there could also be problems – the kind of problems some young
couples could never have foreseen. Pat Warnes recalls:*

We were married in 1949 in North London. We'd been engaged for
nine months, and going out for nine months before that. My
husband had been an apprentice lithographic engineer before he
joined the RAF, and when he came out, he still had a couple of
years' apprenticeship to finish. I worked in the office of the printing
company, and that's how we met.

As there was, even in 1949, very little accommodation, my mother
asked if we'd like to have a couple of rooms in their house. It was a
large Victorian terraced house, with plenty of rooms and more than
enough stairs. We turned my bedroom on the first floor into a
kitchen/living room, then up some stairs to the shared bathroom
(with some tenants of my mother's who had been bombed out in
1944 and never moved back), then up more stairs to the attic which
was to be our bedroom. Our kitchen had a deep white Butler sink
with one cold tap, and a second-hand gas cooker on four little legs,
with no regulo. It must have come out of the Ark, but as I couldn't
cook, I could always blame the stove.

As I'd been an only child, my mother still expected to take first
place in my thoughts and affections. My father had his own catering
business, which meant that he was out most evenings, and my
mother expected to share those evenings with us. She would also try
to find some way of getting me to herself, and I remember that soon
after we married my husband had a bout of malaria (as a result of
serving in India), and my mother kept on about how much fuss he
was making. She was very generous to us, but it was hard going.

*The only solution for Mr and Mrs Warnes seemed to be to move.
However, finding, and affording, somewhere else, was difficult – and
when they eventually got there, other problems were in store:*

We saved for six years. My husband worked two days a week from
7am–6pm, and the other three days from 7am–11pm, so that the
overtime money could be saved. I did housework for my mother, and
typing for my father's business. We grew mushrooms in the cellar,
and did printing on a little Adana machine. Eventually we were able
to put down a deposit on a three-bedroom, semi-detached house in
Enfield in a cul-de-sac with a golf course at the end of the road. This
house cost £3,200, or £14 per month in repayments.

Word had got round our road that a factory-worker with three young children and NO CAR was moving in, and I don't know what the neighbours expected. I'd never encountered 'keeping up with the Joneses' until I moved to the suburbs. I think that the only thing which saved us from absolute isolation was when my father drove down the road in his Jaguar. We saved hard to buy nice curtains for the front room, and bought splendid red velvet, lined ones from Maples. Within two months four houses in the road had lined velvet curtains. We found out later that most of the cars belonged to reps, and were firms' cars anyway – and these people had the cheek to look down on my husband who had a great skill, simply because he didn't have a car.

For Mr and Mrs Warnes, the answer to their housing problem was back-breaking work to save the down-payment on a mortgage. Other couples were luckier, inheriting houses when their relatives died, and able to sell them to finance a move. Cedric Parcell and his wife did this – and Mr Parcell's account shows, in passing, how desperate people were to buy houses in the early 1950s:
We didn't expect to get more than a few hundred for my father's house in Hull. But we were in for a pleasant surprise. We sold the house without the services of an estate agent, and when we advertised it we were overwhelmed with the response. For a week the phone never stopped ringing and, as we showed round one prospective buyer after another, we heard a succession of heart-rending tales as would-be purchasers pleaded with us to sell. The offers went higher and higher, and we couldn't believe our luck. A local firm of printers eventually brought the bidding to an end, pinning us down to £1,250 – twice what my father had paid for it in 1922, and leaving us with a very manageable mortgage. In general the cost of living had risen only moderately on 1939 prices, but a sure sign of the coming inflation was the way the house prices were beginning to escalate.

Moving to a house we'd chosen for ourselves made us feel that we'd taken a big step up the ladder of home ownership. What little money we had to spare went into improving it, and we began to learn what DIY was all about (although I don't think the expression was in use then).

DIY was a background – or sometimes foreground – to life in many homes. Susan Cran writes of her father 'inventing amazing built-in cupboards to fit difficult corners and spaces', and doing decorating and

other jobs around the home. John Tyrrell also remembers his parents'
home-decorating sessions:

So far as we children were concerned, it was like watching them go
into quarantine. The room in question was declared out of bounds to
'small fry', and rolls of paper, tins of paint, brushes and paste-
buckets would disappear into it. I think most of the work must have
been done at night, after we went to bed: I remember mysterious
crashes and muffled thuds (which I excitedly put down to ghosts),
and there was sometimes a strained atmosphere next day at
breakfast. After a few days the room was reopened, seeming bigger
and brighter than before, and with a seductive smell of wallpaper
paste. The smell gave me a taste for a time for papier-mâché
modelling, but my mother always made me use flour paste, and after
a while that went mouldy and stank, which was not the same thing at
all.

From home decorating, my father moved on to more ambitious
DIY – and I have to say, his success was mixed. He was good at
mending locks and door-handles, for example, but never mastered
bookshelves. He always claimed that his finished bookshelves –
planks laid on bricks – were invented out of poverty or a desire to
use simple materials in a simple way, but nowadays, having struggled
to make shelves myself, I suspect other reasons. He was a dab hand
at demolition. He knocked out the wall between the kitchen and the
scullery, hoping to make a huge 'farmhouse' kitchen, and we all
waded through brick dust and plaster rubble for what seemed like
weeks. I remember he was well into the work when he said (I hope
he was joking), 'I wonder if this is a supporting wall'. Later, he took
to knocking holes in the outside walls to make windows. Our house
was made from stone blocks the size of pillows, and my father's
enthusiasm with the sledgehammer, combined with five young
children running around outside, must have caused my mother many
a premature grey hair.

Decorating was one of the few household jobs which in those days,
married couples commonly shared. In general, attitudes to 'men's' and
'women's' work were far more rigid then than now. Pat Warnes
remembers:

For the most part my husband was working, but he did enjoy
gardening and decorating. I guess he must have changed a nappy
some time, but I can't remember, and he very seldom washed up or
did housework. But then he couldn't do everything, and my

generation was brought up to believe that the wife did the housework. When I see my children's spouses now, I marvel at the shared workload.

One of the DIY tasks John Tyrrell's father undertook ('mercifully, with help from experts', his son comments) was plumbing. The bathroom had to be refitted; a proper water-heating system had to be installed, replacing the ancient bathroom geyser and feeding the kitchen (which until then had only one cold-water tap); there was even the possibility of central heating. In other houses, and particularly those in the depths of the countryside, people were not so lucky. For Catharine D. Clarke, who lived in the 1950s with a husband and three children under five in rural Kent, hot water was a priority and an endless worry: The only water supply was a well in the garden. Wash day was a nightmare: endless trips to the well with buckets, to fill an enormous stone copper in the garden shed which was heated by any wood and rubbish that I could collect. Rinsing was practically non-existent. Bath nights were another problem. During the summer, water had to be heated on a Primus stove and an old single oil burner. So it was bucket-trips to the well and a long wait for the water to heat. We had an old hip-bath, and it was all done systematically. Baby first, then Daughter Two, Daughter One and finally me – by which time the water was grubby and cold. My husband made his own arrangements: usually a strip wash from a bucket.

Catharine Clarke ends her letter, with feeling: My life today is so different. We have a lovely house with every mod. con. imaginable, and a car each. When I hear youngsters bemoaning the fact that they don't have things like washing machines, I often think back to my early days on that farm – not with regret but with relief that it's all over. The good old days? You can keep them! Yours in comfort and luxury . . .

The mention of washing machines would strike a particular chord with Wyn and Harold Mack. Mr Mack writes: In about 1954 Gamages of London were advertising an electric clothes-washing machine: a round, barrel-like cylinder with an agitator. It was the first time I'd ever seen such a gadget advertised, for what seemed a reasonable sum of money. At that time Wyn was washing clothes in a big sink in the kitchen, using a washboard – just one step ahead from the way our mothers had washed their clothes.

(They had both used a big, oval, corrugated steel bath on a wooden stand with soap, washboard and scrubbing brush.) With three children to wash for, one a baby, as well as my dirty work-clothes and coveralls, washday for Wyn was an all-day chore. Well, we bought that electric washing machine, added a hand-operated wringer which we already had, and this was a great help. It was a 'first' for us, and was probably the first electric washing machine for miles around. It did a good job, but, being a new gadget, was not too well engineered, and I spent a fair amount of time fitting new belts and pulleys to keep it going.

Kath Price recalls all too well what hard work it was without a washing machine:
I had three small girls then, all under four years old. I had to wash their dresses and socks every night before going to bed, and iron them ready for the next day. I knitted and darned in those days, and made little dresses from hand-me-downs.

Harold Mack also remembers another household appliance, which, like a washing machine, is now taken for granted but was then a novelty:
A sign of the times, a small refrigerator, our first, had been installed a few months before by the council – for the sum, if I remember rightly, of 1/3d (about 6p) a week, paid along with the rent. Again, we were one of the first to obtain one of these modern gadgets, a great boon to Wyn and the household. Actually that fridge was not working properly, and as we'd no experience of such things, it was two years before we complained and got another new one supplied, where the freezing compartment (big enough to contain one pint of icecream) would keep the icecream frozen. One lives and learns.

What did people do before fridges? Jean Gostelow points out:
Except for icecream, there were no chilled or frozen foods in those days. Yoghurt was unheard-of. We made the meals we needed as we needed them, and ate food fresh. If my mother ever heard about frozen vegetables, not to mention such modern monstrosities as frozen chips or frozen sponge cakes, she'd be spinning in her grave.

Rena Brewin adds:
We kept milk fresh by standing it in a bowl of water with a cloth over, and there was a meat-safe in the greenhouse at the back of the house.

Another household gadget, standard today, was still a luxury for many people in the 1950s. Harold Mack explains – and describes a cheap alternative:

For the nine years we lived in that house we were never rich enough to have a telephone. At that time it took a lot of money, and at least six months from application, to have the phone installed. My sister and her husband lived about two miles away, and were the only people we knew who had a home phone. We had to make outgoing calls (not very often deemed necessary), from a pay phonebox near by. Usually, for communication, a letter was sent – and at that time, if my memory serves me correctly, it cost 2½d (about 1p). The service was very good: a local letter sent in the morning would probably be delivered the same day.

Rosemary Ridyard and Susan Cran recall some other features of 1950s houses, which might seem rather quaint today. Rosemary Ridyard writes:

Central heating and double glazing did not exist in ordinary houses. Fitted carpets hadn't arrived. We had carpet squares in the main rooms, with surrounds of wood or lino, which had to be dusted, scrubbed and polished. Fitted kitchens were unknown, and bathrooms were functional, usually black and white and devoid of showers.

Susan Cran adds:

My aunt and uncle lived on the top floor of my grandmother's house. At one point they redecorated the kitchen, and I remember my amazement (as a child) at the Formica worktop. They also got one of those tall, white kitchen dressers with sliding glass doors in the top and little paintings or transfers in yellow and red on the glass. It seemed so exciting and modern then. Now you see them outside the worst of cheap junk shops in slummy areas!

3

COUNTRY LIFE

'Perfick! Just perfick!'
Pa Larkin in H. E. Bates'
The Darling Buds of May

During the war, the fact that Britain was an island provided vital protection against invasion. But it also prevented the free flow of imports. Farming was an essential industry – so much so that it was a 'reserved occupation', acceptable as an alternative to fighting in the forces. So long as we were careful, our farmers were able to grow and raise enough food to feed the population: a remarkable achievement.

In some parts of the country, wartime farms had concentrated on a single crop or a single purpose; grain in East Anglia, sheep on the Welsh hills and Yorkshire Moors, fruit in Worcestershire and Kent. Other farms were small and mixed. They set their stamp on country areas until well into the 1950s – and also created the picture of a kind of idyll of country life which Val Hastings remembers as a small child – and which, as she says, the Larkin books and TV programmes so amiably celebrated.

My grandparents had a rented farm with five fields in Hereford. When 'The Darling Buds of May' was on TV recently, it reminded me so much of the farm. The dresses I wore were the same as the younger Larkin daughter. We went hop-picking instead of fruit-picking, but the countryside was very similar. My Dad worked in Birmingham, but I had glorious weekends and holidays on the farm. We had candles on saucers to go upstairs to bed, and feather mattresses made by my two aunts when they plucked all the chickens, geese and turkeys. They grew apples for Bulmers Cider, and kept cows, pigs, and hens. I used to collect all the eggs every morning. I regret the passing of this kind of life before my daughter had a chance to see it for herself, but that's progress I suppose.

19

Mrs C.S. Thornton remembers:
Our farm, like those of all our neighbours, had no mains electricity, water or sewage disposal. Calor Gas provided lighting in the downstairs rooms and we went to bed by candlelight. My mother cooked on an Aga, the oven of which came in handy for reviving premature lambs, and she made our own clotted cream. We had our own water supply from our own spring. It was crystal clear and cold, and the spring lasted through a dry summer when the local reservoir started to dry up, causing those on the 'mains' to have their supply cut.

After the war, the housing shortage in towns and cities drove many young couples to rent what they could find in the country. For such 'incomers', life was by no means idyllic. Joan Harper comments:
Having been born and brought up in London, I found life in the country a completely new experience. I had to fill and clean oil lamps each morning. I cooked with a coal range, which meant I had to clean the flues, blacklead the stove and whiten the hearth. Water had to be brought in from a standpipe outside. The toilet was in an outdoor shed: a new departure for me. I had a baby daughter, and nappies had to be rinsed outside at the standpipe, in a bath. Shopping was difficult and I had to take my pram and baby on the train to get supplies. The most amazing part of all this was that although we were in the country with no convenience, we were still only about twenty miles from London. In those days when night fell there was total darkness. No lights once we went outside the door, yet in the distance we could see the sky lit up with the glow of London.

Rhoda Woodward gives more detail:
In 1950 I was living with my husband, a daughter of two and a baby son in a tied farm cottage in a small hamlet in Oxfordshire. The accommodation consisted of a living room, a bedroom and an attic. There was only one door, which opened on to the living room. A wooden screen on the left gave the semblance of a hall, and there was a door on the right leading to the stairs. In the opposite corner was a cupboard under the stairs which was a kind of pantry. This housed a bucket of fresh water, among other things, as all the water had to be fetched from a pump at the end of the yard.

At the other side of the room was a big old chimney corner and an open range with a side oven. There was also a brick bread-oven, but

I never had the courage to use it, as I believe it had to be filled with faggots of wood and then, when they were all burned, the whole lot raked out. I managed very well with the range and the oven. I used to cook on the hobs and had two flat iron bars to stand the saucepans on if I wanted them over the flame. The chimney was very wide, and if I didn't remember to keep a lid on all the pans I could end up with a sprinkling of soot in with the vegetables.

A small wash-house had been built on by the front door. Inside was a big, shallow sink which had a drain but no tap. In the corner was a built-in brick copper, which held six buckets of water. Often my husband would fill it for me on the Sunday evening ready for me to light on Monday morning. (This was frowned on by some of our older neighbours: in those days men were not supposed to do 'women's work'.) It was surprising how quickly the old copper used to come to the boil, as it was mostly rubbish – old newspapers, cardboard boxes and sticks we collected – which I used to heat the water. There was a fire-hole with a small iron door at the bottom, and the flames went up and round the copper bowl that held the water. All 'whites' had to be boiled and then rinsed, with a squeeze of the 'blue bag' added to the last rinse.

I kept a large saucepan on the hob, filled with water so that there was always hot water for washing up etc. I used to put the water from the hot-water bottles in that saucepan: we never wasted water. We had a large soft-water tank by the door. If it rained a lot and the tank began to overflow, we would don macs and fill up the copper and every available vessel we could find, so that the lovely soft water did not go to waste.

It was a mile each way to the two nearest villages. We had to walk down to them to shop or to catch a bus into Banbury, our nearest town. Food was still rationed, and you had to register your books with the grocer. We would take our list to the shop and the groceries would be delivered for the weekend. Another young couple lived opposite, and we used to walk down together or take turns taking the orders. If we needed something really urgent one of us would have the children and the other would go to the village on a bicycle. Meat was brought round in a small van twice a week. We usually had offal (liver, heart, kidney) in the week, and the two ounces of corned beef allowed by the ration, and a joint of some sort (to the cost of our meat allowance) for the weekend. Milk and bread came together in the Co-op van. The coalman came round once a month. Our coal ration was one hundredweight per week. I had 5/- (25p) a week family allowance; I used to draw the pound once a month and that paid for four bags of coal and a bag of slack or coke which the man let us have 'off ration'. There were often a few coppers left for an icecream when we went out.

Our cottage was on the end of a block of four. A wide yard ran along the front of the houses. The back faced the road. Across the yard was a row of four stone-built sheds. They were a good size, and we could keep our coal, wood, vegetables and bikes in there with plenty of room to spare. The farmer used to let us borrow a horse and cart on a Saturday afternoon in autumn, and we went round the fields and gathered a load of wood. One year he had an old tree cut down, and it was shared among the workers. The man who lived next door had a circular saw, and all the men got together on a Sunday morning and sawed up the logs.

Each cottage had a good-sized piece of garden. The plots were wider than the houses, so next door's garden was in front of our house and ours was further along. Past our garden and along the side almost to the top was another row of four stone buildings: the privies. Each had a red brick floor and a wooden box across the width of the little room. There was a hinged seat with a hole in it, which you lifted up to remove the bucket underneath. Every three weeks or so, the men could be seen digging a hole in the garden on a Saturday afternoon. They would then empty the buckets late in the evening when they came back from the pub.

Although machines were used for some of the work, most farms in the early 1950s still depended on human muscle-power, and many still used horses. Mrs C.S. Thornton remembers that all the farms in her area of Somerset kept carthorses as well as tractors – and that 'Smart' was a favourite name for a horse. She tells of a local character, 'a large ex-farmer, ruddy with cider-drinking, who rode his carthorse round the lanes'. As for human muscles, farmwork was still labour-intensive. Mrs G. Dix says:

All the harvesting of peas, beans, potatoes and fruit was done by hand. Sugar beet was pulled up and topped also by hand. It was hard work in unpleasant (usually muddy, frosty) weather.

Norman Green contrasts corn-harvesting, then and now:

Many of the smaller farms harvested their wheat with a 'binder'. That is, the corn was cut by a machine resembling a giant mower, which also tied it into bundles called sheaves. The bundles were propped in 'stooks' to dry before being made into a stack for threshing (separating grain from straw) later on. An agricultural contractor usually brought a big machine for this work in the winter. Nowadays, the combine harvester eliminates all this handling and separates the grain from the straw as the corn is cut. This is why many hedges have now been cleared away: to give the giant combines a clear run of a big single field. Years ago, fields were much smaller.

There were other jobs, just as back-breaking as harvesting, but lonelier and far less pleasant. John Wilton remembers, as a boy, pigeon-scaring at sowing-time: running up and down and shouting, just as people had done for centuries before him. Mr E.H. describes pulling tares (wild grain) from the fields by hand, a far more laborious job then than now, when chemical weedkillers restrict their growth. And Norman Green talks of a situation which became particularly gruesome, thanks to human interference with the environment:

On country holidays after the war, I had met and become friendly with people working on agricultural pest control. And through them I met rabbit trappers and gamekeepers. I remember going with a trapper to a field heavily plagued with rabbits. It was a thirty-three-acre field, like a square of 400 by 400 yards. On two sides of it was woodland. From the edge of the field to about twenty to thirty yards in, the corn was gnawed away: the stalks were short, the grain nearly gone. It looked almost like a man going bald. This was the damage caused by rabbits (calculation – if the crop left intact is, say, 360 yards by 360, that is only twenty-seven acres of good corn in a thirty-three acre field). The cash loss was immense. There were thousands of rabbits to the acre; war on rabbits was unceasing, and rabbit-meat was a favourite food for humans.

What happened, then, to alter things? Well, it is thought that in 1954 someone deliberately brought, from Australia perhaps, germs of the rabbit disease myxomatosis. However the disease started, it went through British rabbits like a plague. Dying rabbits, looking as though they had leprosy or some other horrible complaint, were crawling in millions everywhere in the country. Their verminous, stinking carcases had to be gathered, burned and buried. No farmer escaped such work. When the epidemic was over, rabbits had nearly disappeared.

A year or two after the myxomatosis plague, I revisited the same field. It was amazing. The corn stood high and thick right up to the edges of the field. Only people who witnessed scenes like this can appreciate what a boon to farmers it was when the rabbit population was thinned right down, to one-hundredth or one-thousandth of the old numbers. Even so, this was not much comfort to the people who had to gather the carcases, or to those who had relied on, and enjoyed, rabbit-meat till then.

Despite such horrors, and for all the heavy work and lack of convenience, country life in the 1950s does seem to have had its advantages. Many people found it, if not idyllic, at least satisfying. The rewards were often not tangible – but they still haunt people's minds. 'At apple-pressing time,' says Mrs G. Dix, 'the smell of apples from the nearby cider factory invaded everywhere.' To grow up in rural surroundings could be especially fulfilling. Mrs C.S. Thornton remembers hitching rides, as a child, on the wooden hay-wagons at harvest-time – and later, a kind of placid Somerset version of the US Wild West:

I used to enjoy rounding up the cows for milking, driving them down the lane mounted on my pony. There was very little traffic on the road, and what there was was local. No one minded being held up, and I knew the drivers.

Pat Freestone and Carol Williams look back on their country childhoods with particular affection. For Pat Freestone at eight years old, life as an almost unending whirl of excitement:

I was being brought up in the country, where my mother and father had settled after the war, with my sister and two brothers. Dad grew most vegetables in our garden; he also kept chickens, and for a change of meat we would go out with a couple of ferrets and a terrier to catch rabbits. Also when the corn was being cut by a thresher and piled into 'wigwams', rabbits would run out, to be caught by men and their dogs: we always ate well that day.

Ration books were still in use. Lots of things were scarce, but the situation was accepted and acceptable. Oh, the feeling of achievement at having found a 'moggy's' (moorhen's) nest and borne the contents ever so carefully home for Mum! The joy of helping smallholder Mr Frampton milk his cows, before I went to school, and of learning their names and tasting the fresh, warm milk! He paid me well, 2/- (10p) I recall. Then, to earn extra money, I did my Gran's housework for her. Gran was my mother's mother, and lived upstairs. She paid me 9d (3½p) for 'making ducks' puddles', as she would sometimes unkindly say. But as I brushed her long, grey hair, she told me stories of how country life used to be when she was young: of pawnshops, and of making clothes for her ten children from washed white flour-sacks.

Carol Williams was a little older, and her memories are of a slightly different kind:
I was born in 1944 in a place called Rhydyfelin, near Pontypridd. In those days it was very rural, unlike now, when housing has been built on the beautiful hills. My friends and I spent a great deal of time out-of-doors, and there was absolutely no fear then of being molested. During the summer months, we'd play in the field at the back of our garden where we'd be surrounded by all sorts of wild flowers. As the area was a bit boggy, a favourite flower called lady's-smock (*cardamine pratensis*) used to grown there in profusion. Needless to say, I regularly used to come home covered in mud.

On Sunday mornings my friend used to call for me and we'd walk up the mountain to a village called Eglwsilan, which was over the other side. It was quite a long walk, but worth it because of the beauty of the countryside. I'll always remember one pretty lane: it was overhung by tall trees and, halfway down, a stream ran underneath. The water was crystal clear and I spent ages there mesmerised by it as it flowed over the rocks, forming little waterfalls as it went. (All that has gone now, unfortunately, as the farmer sold the land for housing. But I still have my memories.)

It was a pleasure to go to school during the summer, for there was so much to see on the way. There was a school bus of course, but I rarely used it, except in bad weather. School was quite a distance away but that didn't deter me, and I always saw something interesting on the way. Above my parents' house was the old Glamorganshire Canal (now filled in), and this stretched all the way from Merthyr to Cardiff. The walk to school was pleasant, quiet and deserted. It was quite safe – but even so, when I approached the feeder stream, I used to rush past in case it sucked me in!

4

FOOD

'Please, sir, I want some more.'
Oliver in Charles Dickens'
Oliver Twist

Queen Mary Tudor said that after she had died, people would find the word 'Calais' on her heart. For any Briton alive at the start of the 1950s, a more likely word might be 'austerity'. It was baffling. We had won the war. We had then survived five further years of grinding hardship, tightening our belts in the causes of national reconstruction and the building of a fairer and better society. And yet, in the home at least, many aspects of life seemed grim.

Rationing puzzled ordinary people most of all. During the war, there had been good reasons to put up with shortages. But why did they persist, after so many years of peace? In the early 1950s, clothes and food were still rationed – and of the two, it was the apparent injustice of food-rationing that hit hardest. Irene Pugh remembers visiting Germany in 1952:

I was totally unprepared for the abundance of food displayed in the shops. (The Germans had discontinued food rationing in 1948.) I was able to buy and eat my first bananas since 1939. There was so much choice in the shops, even with sweets, that it made me wonder who had really won the war.

Jane Fabb, visiting Germany a year later with her friend Annie, gives the same story an even sharper twist:

While we were there, we feasted on goodies yet unknown in Britain, and were given food-parcels to bring home 'for the poor little English girls'. My father, who'd been through two world wars, was furious when we arrived home with these little packages.

26

For anyone too young to know what food-rationing was like (and for anyone older who will need no reminding), this account by Molly Schuessele explains how it worked:

Everybody had to register with a retailer for meat, groceries, sweets. Everybody was given a ration book. Each book bore the name of the customer and the name and address of the retailer. There was a page of coupons for each item, stamped as the rations were collected. Retailers had to keep an account of all rations, in the same way as they kept accounts of their takings. This made a lot of work. In those days addition was done with brain, pen and paper: there were no calculators, and the only 'computers' were the fingers on one's hands.

Apart from rationed items, there were goods which were simply scarce. News went round the housewives that such-and-such a butcher or fishmonger, grocer or sweet shop was having a delivery of something scarce but not rationed. Immediately a queue would form outside that shop. On a system of 'first come, first served', the goods were dealt out. In the butcher's it was offal and sausages or a chunk of beef or pork dripping. Liver, I remember, was prized beyond rubies, and sometimes pigs' heads or sheep's heads were available.

Sweet rationing was strange. Children's ration books had more coupons than adults' books, and older children could go to the sweet shop and buy their ration with their pocket-money. Things like gobstoppers, sherbet bags and chewing gum were barely rationed at all. Fruit sweets and toffee were tightly rationed, and chocolates were as rare as gold. No thought was given to the effect of the sugar on children's teeth. It was thought so necessary for children's growth, that well-meaning adults often gave up their sweet ration for the children, who lapped and crunched it up.

Clothes coupons could be saved up and used all at once. Families used to donate their clothes coupons so that a bride and her bridesmaids could have lovely dresses, and the groom and best man new suits.

Sometimes rationing was little more than an inconvenience. When Phyllis Webb and her husband married in 1953, they went on honeymoon to Perram North in Cornwall – and their first outing had to be to Newquay to pick up their emergency ration books. Other stories, like this from Stella McLeish, seem more amusing now than they did at the time:

It was early in the summer of 1950. We set out to a farm near

Bradford to buy strawberries for jam, having saved the money and the sugar with great effort. Then, when we'd got all the children to bed and hulled and washed the strawberries, we discovered that we hadn't a big enough pan. My husband had the brilliant idea of using an old gas boiler that we'd used to boil the washing until we'd bought a small electric one. We put in the strawberries and the sugar and lit the gas. My husband did the stirring while I got the jars ready. Hours later the strawberry jam still wouldn't jell – I think because we couldn't turn the gas up high enough – and about 2am we had to admit defeat. You can imagine the task we then faced when we had to bail out the great sticky mess and clean the boiler. But what seemed a major tragedy to us was that we'd wasted our money and our precious sugar.

When food was scarce, people improvised. Susan Cran tells how her mother mixed butter and margarine together to eke out the butter – and how her father hated it. John Tyrrell remembers 'biscuits' for tea made by sandwiching icecream wafers round a smear of 'chocolate' spread made with cornflour, cocoa and water. Anne Filkin remembers mashing up parsnips with banana essence to make 'banana sandwiches', and says it was another ten years before she could bring herself to eat parsnips again as a vegetable. Rhoda Woodward tells of other, more palatable, dishes:

We made meat puddings, hash and stews with our corned beef ration. A pan of fried onions with thick gravy, served up with vegetables, made a good meal when there wasn't any meat. Batter made with dried egg or one fresh egg, with sausages (cut up small to go further), bacon or corned beef added to make a main course, or with fruit, jam or even syrup (which was sometimes available) as a pudding, was a good filling stand-by. We grew most of our own vegetables and rented an allotment, so we were able to manage very well. I made jams and pickles, bottled fruit in large Kilner jars and salted down kidney beans. We had a good supply of milk from the farm, and kept it standing in cold water during the summer.

The allotment movement, to which Rhoda Woodward refers, had been a godsend during the war, allowing town-dwellers to 'Dig for Victory' by growing their own fresh vegetables. Now it came into its own again, easing the strain of rationing for many families. Cedric Parcell's memory of its pleasures is typical:

There were allotments on the railway land behind the house and I rented one, growing vegetables and soft fruit. We made jam from our own blackcurrants and bottled our own gooseberries, and when I brought home the first crop of home-grown potatoes they had a flavour better than any we ever bought from the greengrocer.

In towns, scarce food could also be eked out by eating at 'National Restaurants', which had been set up by the government at the beginning of the war, and survived for twenty years. John Tyrrell remembers eating macaroni cheese (for 2/-: 10p) in the Oxford National Restaurant as a student in 1959. Colin Coupland goes into more detail:
When you went in you went to the pay-desk first, selected your meal from the menu, paid, and were given different-coloured discs for each item. White was for potatoes, green for peas, red for carrots, blue for fish, yellow for meat and so on. Then you went upstairs, took a tray and went along the counter. As you handed over your coloured discs, you received each item from the serving-girls.

In the countryside, people relied less on such efficient, if drab, government establishments. Valerie Heath remembers the rich, good milk of the 1940s and early 1950s – and the day that richness stopped, by order:
There were several farms in our village. In the mornings, but especially late afternoons, children would be sent with canisters of various shapes and sizes to collect the milk, fresh that day. My uncle had a farm, isolated in the Yorkshire Wolds, and came into the valley on his milk round. He had several churns on his van, and would ladle out the milk in the street, but usually took it into houses. He stopped at our house for his dinner, and received innumerable cups of tea and gossip on his round, dropping in on us for a last cup when my father got home from work.

One day I got in from school, and my uncle was already there. He asked me to drink a cup of milk and tell him what I thought of it. 'Like school milk,' I said. 'Not very nice.' He heaved a sigh. Pasteurisation wasn't going to do him any good. It must have been hygiene regulations. His milk soon came in bottles, the waves of chattering children with their canisters stopped trooping down the village street, and his Land Rover lost the smell of sweet, whole milk.

Valerie Heath also describes how her father and mother kept the family well fed, even during the deepest days of rationing:
When my father came home after the war he dug our garden and

another two that belonged to old ladies in our terrace. He made a pigsty and a chicken-run, and grew vegetables for all three houses. He used to save the seeds from year to year. When things got better we also had a row of sweet peas. We never bought vegetables or fruit, indeed we couldn't, as the village shops didn't sell them.

The chickens used to come by carrier in boxes, as day-old, fluffy yellow chicks. As they weakly padded and cheeped, holding the box gave a funny sensation. At this point there was also some sort of secret, tense negotiation with the shopkeeper over the road about the oatmeal they ate. It must have been something to do with rationing. Helped by the pigs, the chickens ate all the food-scraps from the three houses. They had to be fed most days, and the eggs had to be collected. This was not as exciting as collecting them on my uncle's farm, as his hens were allowed to ramble at will, and laid their eggs in the most unlikely places. Because you never knew how long an egg had been laid, breaking the shell could sometimes bring a nasty surprise. Every six months or so our chicken-pen would be moved round the garden. Things are never as big as one remembers, but it must have measured ten by twenty yards. During the laying season some of the eggs were preserved in isinglass to help us through the winter. My mother didn't much like the dried egg, and used it as little as possible. From time to time we killed, plucked, drew and ate one of the chickens. In those days, chicken was a great treat.

My grandfather was a farmer and my father knew about pigs. We used to have three at a time. One always disappeared after a few weeks (I don't remember where), and the other two were fattened up for meat. As good building-materials were expensive or scarce, probably both, the sty was a makeshift contraption and, particularly when the pigs were young, they used to escape. We spent a lot of time running after them. My father worked for a butcher, and would kill, dehair, butcher and salt the meat. He sold the gammon to the butcher for the use of his facilities. My mother used to catch the blood and make it into black pudding. The bacon hung from hooks in the kitchen ceiling and in the cupboard under the stairs. Years after we stopped doing this, the cupboard still had a faint smell of salted bacon. The fat was cooked and recooked to render it down to dripping, and the bones and other remains were boiled and stripped to make into brawn.

We used to get milk and butter from the farm. When we went there, we sometimes used to help churn the butter. What a monotonous job!

In many ways, we were well-off for food. My mother had been a cook before she married, and could do wonders with next to nothing. As a boy my father had more or less lived on pastry. Each week his mother, sisters and sisters-in-law had done a marathon bake, entirely covering a huge table. We had no fancy breakfast cereals in those days (or indeed, any at all), but at breakfast, and at every other meal, there were pies, tarts, scones or cake. At the end of baking, my mother would roll lard into the leftover pastry and cook it. She and my father had a long-running joke about whether the result was called 'sad cake' or 'oven-bottom cake'.

We used to have lots of dishes where meat was stretched. A roly-poly filled with meat and onions was a great favourite. Yorkshire puddings were often eaten before the meal with gravy, and sometimes afterwards with a sprinkling of sugar or golden syrup. Cubes of bread with hot milk and sugar were another favourite. Sometimes, but not every week, my mother would bake bread, which we loved. We had a lot of dishes on toast, and made the toast by holding bread on the end of the toasting fork over the fire.

The countryside offered another source of cheap, not to say free, food – at least for a time. Norman Green writes:
Rabbit-trapping must have been an occupation in Britain since Roman times. The countryside was alive with rabbits in a manner unbelievable to people of the 1990s: countless thousands for every one seen nowadays. Until myxomatosis (and the banning of gin-traps) put an end to the trade in 1954, a rabbit-trapper would have set out each evening with about 50 iron traps with spring-operated jaws, for putting down the entrances to rabbit-holes. From the hedge-banks and woodlands, there were clear trails or 'runs' along which the rabbits passed into the crops. Wire snares in the form of nooses held up on thin sticks were placed along these 'runs'. Hundreds of snares were set. The rabbits mostly came out at night. Early next morning, the trapper inspected his traps and snares and collected all the rabbits caught.

In the early years of the 1950s, Joan Cutner was in charge of catering for special diets at her local hospital. She says:
Life was still very much 'post-war'. We were still using tinned and dried eggs, and mock cream made from milk and gelatine. Cakes and dishes made with butter and cream were still a luxury. We made the most of what we had and didn't waste a thing. The hospital waste

went to the pigs. Even now I hate to throw away food, and am appalled when my daughter throws away an apple when there's only a small bruise on it: you can always cut off the bruised part.

In the hospital, food was pretty basic for both patients and staff, but there was plenty of filling, for example potatoes and bread. Fresh eggs were available about once a week; otherwise we used canned whole eggs, or dried eggs, for such things as scrambled egg and cakes. Meringues and cake-icings were made from powdered egg white called Merriwhite (which can now again be bought in the shops). Although we had fresh milk, delivered in churns, we still used dried milk to eke it out. I well remember the frustration of trying to make custard with dried milk. If you weren't careful, it would be lumpy – and even worse, would burn on the bottom of the pan. You can strain out lumps, but not a burnt taste.

It was hard to make meat, fish and cheese go round from the amounts allocated to us in the diet section, and I can remember stripping cooked chicken until there wasn't a scrap of meat left on the bone.

As the decade wore on, however, things became easier. Overseas trade picked up, and supplies became more plentiful. Food rationing was finally abolished in 1954. But even before then, cracks in the system were beginning to appear – as this story from Norman Green shows:
In early 1953, I was in Scotland, sent on a job by my employers. I was staying in lodgings in Uddingston, an outer fringe of Glasgow, near the birthplace of the explorer David Livingstone. One day I went into a little corner shop, and asked for my weekly ration of bacon: if I remember rightly, some small amount like four ounces. The grocer put my allotted amount on the scales. We were alone in the shop. He said, 'If you could have more, would you want it?' I replied, 'I'd be glad of more, but I don't want to do anything illegal.' He said, 'The war's been over eight years. The farmers are getting back to the pre-war levels of production. There's plenty of bacon, at least round here.' I said in that case I'd have a good helping, so that we could celebrate in the house where I was staying. I think I bought something like twenty-four ounces, and gave them to my landlady and fellow lodger.

In that shadowy little shop, on a day as winter was ending, it was as though a great light shone. This was a watershed. Fourteen years after the war with Hitler had started, it looked as if the years of hardship and scarcity were really about to end.

When rationing finally did end, other people had a similar feeling of excitement. In books and comics of the time, people were always celebrating happy events with a 'great big feed' – and now it looked as if these dream-binges might be possible in real life too. Rena Brewin recalls how, as a seven-year-old, she was suddenly told that she could buy as many sweets as she wanted, and wondered whether to borrow a 'gidgy' (a cart made from old wood and pram-wheels) from the boys up the road. Unfortunately no one told her the one remaining problem: that her 'sweetie penny' would still only buy the same amount as it had before. Other children, also too young to remember life without rationing, were doomed to disappointment in other ways, as Frederick Walkden remembers:

The first appearance of bananas in the village nearly caused a riot. They were sold, a pound only to each family, so that everyone could have a taste. A couple of years ago, a friend of mine told me that when her two children had bananas for the first time, they didn't like them, and spat them out.

Adults, who knew what they'd been missing, had a rather better time of it – like Philomena Cooper (then Corporal Tonge of the WAAF) and a friend, 'somewhere in Northumberland' (as wartime news-bulletins used to put it):

I remember butter being almost if not *the* last thing to come off ration in the summer of 1954. I was on a mobile exhibition tour of Northern Command, and we walked into a grocer's shop at coffee-break one Monday, and said, 'What would you say if we asked for one and a half pounds of best butter?' The charming gent behind the counter said, 'Certainly, young ladies'. I can't remember whether this was in Workington or Whitehaven, but I *do* remember that Corporal Audrey Dereham and I blew the whole lot on four fresh cobs warm from the bakery – and we weren't sick either!

Happy days were almost – but not quite – here again. As Maxine Elvey reminds us, years of shortages and 'making do' had had their effect on the British diet and our cooking methods. 'Basic', rather than 'imaginative', is the word that springs to mind:

Food in the 1950s was plainer and more limited. School dinner perhaps typified English cooking at that time. (Incidentally, although they are now a lot better, school dinners had not improved much in the 1970s, when I began teaching.) There were thin, dry slices of gristly beef, moistened with gravy. The meat was like leather. You would chew it for ages, then leave the gristle on the side of your plate. There were slices of Spam and corned beef. Potato was mashed and very lumpy. It used to make me gag – and the thought of it still does. Custard was either very runny or lumpy with strips of skin. There were milk puddings – semolina, sago, tapioca – which I liked.

One of the main differences between then and now was that in the 1950s people used mainly fresh foods, usually local. In London, for example, I think that greengrocers used to go themselves to Covent Garden, fishmongers to Billingsgate, and butchers to Smithfield. There were no distribution lorries like today.

Fruit and vegetables were wrapped in brown paper bags or newspaper. They were often covered in soil. They were not standardised in size as they are today, and I think they really did taste better. There were only seasonal fruit and vegetables, and a few imported things: bananas, oranges, and tangerines and nuts at Christmas. In the summer we used to buy peas and sit on the back step shelling them in the warm sunshine.

At home we always ate brown bread – something very unusual at that time. Probably the only brown loaf was the Hovis. I remember my mother sending me to the local baker's to buy a Hovis. It cost 4¼d (2p). We also used to buy baby Hovises – miniature versions.

At home, we sometimes had tinned food. My mother regularly gave us tinned mangoes and cream. I didn't encounter a fresh mango until I went to India in 1966, though they are common now in shops. We used to eat tinned peaches and cream with our Christmas pudding.

Frozen food came in very gradually during the 1950s. At some point fish fingers were invented, and they soon became a regular part of our diet at home, put under the grill. I never liked them. Frozen peas were the first frozen food we ate regularly. Yoghurt was not eaten much in the 1950s. At first we ate only the sour milk made from the TT (tuberculin tested) milk. Then the milkman began to sell plain yoghurt. But not many people ate it, and unlike today it was never included in school dinners. It was considered a health food, not ordinary fare.

Maxine Elvey ends her letter with a memory absolutely typical of the mid-1950s, when 'treats' of any kind were still in short supply:
My grandparents always had Cadbury's Roses chocolates in the sideboard, always with white stale patches and tasting stale. Either Granpa was given out-of-date chocolates, or they kept them for a long time. At school we sucked Polos, Spangles, Rowntree's Fruit

Gums and Fruit Pastilles. Everybody liked the blackcurrant ones best. Next door to our school was a paper shop selling sweets. There was no talk of sweets being bad for your teeth. However, Mum used to ration sweets. When we were in the infants' school we were given one after breakfast to suck on the way to school. Then we always kept chocolates in a box for Sunday. When people came to see us, or we them, we often took chocolates. (Visiting was much more formal in those days.)

5

SHOPS

'The street outside was full of lip-smacking people.'
Molly Schuessele

Everyone knows that in the last forty years, there has been a revolution in the way we shop. But the sheer size of the change only becomes apparent when we think back to how goods were bought and sold in the days before supermarkets, shopping malls, credit cards and buying-by-phone. For example, Jane Fraser Cross remembers deliveries – which were a vital feature of 1950s shopping, all but disappeared today:

The milkman and breadman called every day, and you paid them at the end of each week. During the week, you used the Co-op or Lipton's, and had your order for food delivered by the shop's van. Saturday you went shopping, and with what money you had left perhaps bought a few treats for when you watched Saturday night's telly.

Rena Brewin goes into more detail:

In those days, there were lots of deliveries to the door: the fruit and veg man with a horse and cart, Daisy Dampwash, the milkman, the baker, the Corona man with lemonade, the crumpet man, the icecream man on Sundays, the grocery boy on his bike from the Co-op. All these were weekly. The knife-grinder, coalman, rag-and-bone-man, vicar and Kleeneze brushman all came at longer intervals.

Rena Brewin also remembers her excitement, as a small girl, at visiting the most up-to-the-minute shop in town, the local Co-op:

It had an overhead system to take money to cashiers in the wooden 'box' in the corner – it used to ping when set off and whir over to the corner. There were seats to sit on until your change came whirring back. Biscuits were in boxes and there was a bacon slicer: you could choose the setting, from thick to thin.

36

Mum used to buy bread checks (tokens) and milk checks to put out for the deliveries, and handed over the list of groceries to be delivered by the boy on his bike with the big basket.

I remember once going shopping on my own for Mum, and chanting 'Half butter and quarter ham 26157' over and over so I wouldn't forget. (26157 was our Co-op dividend number.)

These Co-op dividend numbers were vital for families. Maxine Elvey explains why:
You got so much back for every pound you spent, and when it had built up you could claim it as your 'divi'. The idea was that customers should share in the company's profits. My sister and I often went shopping for small items, and I remember our dividend number to this day: 139499. (I forget phone numbers of friends when they move, but still remember this number, etched in the clear, uncluttered mind of a young child.)

Molly Schuessele left the ATS in 1946, and went to work as manageress of a kind of shop which has now virtually disappeared: a specialist tobacconist's. In those days little was known of the dangers of smoking, and cigarettes were a necessity, a social convention and even a fashion accessory. Until well into the 1950s, they were also hard to come by, as Mrs Schuessele recalls:
The whole stock was kept under the counter, and dished out sparingly. I was courted by many men – not for my charms but for my power over their smoking habits. I got to know my regular customers and which brands they preferred. The white-collar workers liked Players Navy Cut and Capstan Medium or Strong. The posh folks smoked Sobranie or Three Castles, 333 and 555, cigarettes which were slightly more expensive. The working class preferred Woodbines, Tenners Red, Tenners Blue and Players Weights. The cigarettes which were most readily available were Turkish. They were rolled and then flattened, and smelt to high heaven – definitely an acquired taste. Another common kind was mentholated cigarettes, which were supposed to be good for a bad chest and throat.

Pipe tobacco wasn't quite so scarce. Class distinction applied as much to pipe tobaccos as to cigarettes. Old Holborn, a strong smelling tobacco, was a favourite of the working man. More expensive tobaccos were favoured by white-collar workers. Erinmore Flake and Erinmore Rubbed were sweet smelling tobaccos, Capstan Flake and Capstan Rubbed were strong smelling, rather like burning socks.

Molly Schuessele goes on to write in detail of Colchester in the 1940s and 1950s, giving the shop-assistant's-eye view of what shops, and their customers, were like. As with attitudes to cigarette-smoking, how times have changed!

Between 1949 and 1955 I worked in three different shops. The first was a greengrocer, grocer and general stores. The second was a rather higher-class grocer's shop, and the third was a sweet shop and tobacconist's.

The greengrocer's shop was about the last of the old Victorian and Edwardian small shops which sold everything anyone could want, and gave credit to customers – who on the whole were of working class, with a sprinkling of more prosperous people living in the area who shopped there for convenience. Usually it was very busy, very untidy, but the service was excellent. Customers' orders were delivered promptly. The orders were collected from the customers' kitchen doors, by the shop owner, his wife and family. If any customer wanted the order in time to cook the vegetables for dinner, for instance, the order had a cross put against it in the order book, and anybody passing by the shop was prevailed on to hand the order in, where an assistant would get it packed up and the errand boy would deliver it at once. My father also delivered orders. It became a familiar sight around the part of Colchester served by our shop, to see him perched on his errand bike, loaded down with boxes and bags, and with cans of paraffin tied to the handlebars. This type of shop lasted for the first few years of the 1950s.

The superior type of shop I worked in until 1953 was a provision merchant's. Here we sold higher-quality and more expensively packed things. Biscuits were still sold loose, but the bags had the shop's name printed on them. Sugar, flour, rice and other dry goods were also sold loose, but were packed into different-coloured bags. Sultanas and currants were dropped onto the floor and trodden underfoot. Hygiene was still very primitive. There was one stone sink with a cold water tap, and a wooden draining board which should have been scrubbed regularly, but had turned a dirty brown and smelt mouldy. There was a gas ring to heat a kettle, and a thin towel to wipe our hands. Cooked meats, such as ham, Spam and pork brawn, were displayed under a glass counter. There was no refrigeration as we know it today. The bacon slicer was the devil to clean, but we did our best.

Rationing was still on in the early 1950s, and much time was used to count the points coupons. Unlike in our first shop, we did no

canvassing for orders, and delivered very few. Only people living near
by got deliveries, although other similar shops in town did deliver.

The shop was one of a row of small shops. The chemist on the
corner was next to a dry cleaner's, then a tiny fresh-fish shop. The
marble slab took up three quarters of the fish shop, so that if there
were three customers, the shop was full. Mr Shepherd, the
fishmonger, had a job to reach the fish in the middle of the slab. But
his fish was fresh, and according to season, of many varieties. I
especially remember the juicy shrimps and crabs. The shop smelt
strongly of its stock, but Mr Shepherd was meticulous and kept the
slab and the surrounding floor and shelf absolutely spotless. A long
queue would form every day when he got supplies in.

Next to the fish shop was a greengrocer's, which always smelled
pleasantly of apples, onions and carrots. When oranges and bananas
came back after the war, greengrocers took pride in making a
beautiful display of them with other fruit as it came into season.
Next door was a small sweet shop where cigarettes were also sold. A
second-hand clothes shop was next, then a hairdresser's salon where
we could get a shampoo and set for 1/6d (7½p) or a perm for 10/-
(50p). The grocer's was next, and then was a cobbler's, where you
could buy leather goods, straps, dog collars, harness, leather
handbags and handmade leather slippers, as well as having your
shoes and boots repaired.

Next door to the cobbler's was another sweet shop: a small dark
place, one step down inside the door where a bell swung and rang
every time a customer 'minded the step' and came in. Beside the
counter was one small round table with four chairs. Here the
comfortably-off sat and ate icecream from a glass dish, with a silver-
plated teaspoon, for the vast amount of 3d (1½p) or 6d (2½p) per
portion. Mrs Jefferson made her own icecream with goat's milk
which was delivered each morning. The icecream would be ready at
1pm. At 12.30 a queue of chattering people and children in their
school dinner-hour would form. Sharp on one o'clock, Mrs J would
open her door, and the queue passed inside to receive their
halfpenny, penny and tuppenny cornets or wafers, and the 'rich'
would sit and eat theirs from their glass dishes. The street outside
was full of lip-smacking people. It was all over by 1.30pm and
everything was back to normal till next day. Unfortunately, the
Public Health Office investigated Mrs Jefferson, and her kitchen was
found wanting. She had only one sink to wash up in, and that was
her kitchen sink, in which everything including herself was washed.

So her wonderful icecream was no longer permitted. I never heard of anyone getting ill with all this primitive hygiene, as they so often do today with our more stringent rules.

For my third job I left the grocer's and went to the other side of town to the sweet shop and tobacconist. This shop was nearer the centre of town, so the customers were mostly people who worked at the Electricity offices and workshops, and the other shops all round. The sweet shop was quite small. Rationing was still on, so sweets were scarce and cigarettes were hard to come by.

Round the corner from the sweet shop were lots of other shops: a greengrocer, retail and wholesale, a sub post office which also sold stationery and novelties, a baker's shop and a butcher's. Behind the butcher's was a slaughterhouse. The animals were driven on the hoof through the town. It was horrible. The poor things seemed to know what was going to happen, and sometimes ran amok. Imagine that in the heart of a town!

On the opposite corner of St Botolph's Street was a large haberdasher's, draper's and clothing store: a wonderful old-fashioned store, a miniature Selfridges or Harrods. There were three floors. The ground floor sold haberdashery: buttons, tapes, cotton, threads, needles, pins, and knitting patterns, needles and wool. In the early 1950s this part of the store had the 'railway' and the travelling ball to the cash desk. On the second floor were the underwear departments for men, women and children, each department separated by stairways or counters. The counters were long, and were covered with sheets of glass over the mahogany surface. There were a lot of assistants at each counter, and a floor-walker, just like Captain Peacock in 'Are You Being Served' on TV. Along the walls behind the counters were many built-in drawers, some deep, some shallow, some short, some long, holding the various garments on sale. In the ladies' underwear department modesty and discretion were asked for and given. There were curtained-off changing rooms, in which to be fitted for corsets, with a fully trained corsetière at the customers' service. On the third floor were dresses, coats, hats and shoes for ladies, gentlemen and children, each department divided off as before.

This shop was very prosperous and only gave up trading in the late 1960s, when the proprietor retired and modern department stores were coming into being. All its managers, floor-walkers, assistants, storemen, right down to the window cleaner and general dogsbody, were customers in my tobacco shop. The manager in 1953–55 eventually became Mayor of Colchester.

Not everyone bought ready-made clothes, even from shops as magnificent as this one. Maxine Elvey comments:
Most people then used dressmakers. For many women, dressmaking was a way of earning money and working at home. In my teens we had a dressmaker called Mrs Stone. Ladies' suits were made by ladies' tailors, usually men, also often working from home. My uncle was one. I remember brown woollen tweed material in his house, and the ironing board he used to press the clothes as he made them.

Molly Schuessele continues her memory of the shops in 1950s Colchester:
In the High Street there were many shops which have disappeared now. A hardware shop, selling everything you could need for DIY, was next door to Boots the Chemist. Burtons the Tailors and Evans the Outsize Shop were near by. Poyser's, a prestigious bookshop, was next door to a home-made cake shop and café where 'ladies of family' took their elevenses. Further along the High Street were Woolworth's, a small Marks and Spencer's and a large Sainsbury's. Sainsbury's was of particular interest. It was divided into two sections. For dairy produce and meat you queued up (yes almost every time, it was so busy) at one door. You queued for butter (which stood in large slabs on a marble-topped rear counter), margarine, lard and dripping. Then you moved on for cheese and bacon, and then you queued again for meat. I remember that flank of Argentinian beef sold for 6d (2½p) a pound and was delicious. An added bonus was a lovely pot of beef dripping. (No thought then of cholesterol!) After queuing at the meat counter, you walked through a doorway into the next shop to buy other groceries from sales assistants who were trained to weigh up such things as sugar, tea and biscuits – and also to persuade customers to buy anything which was on special offer. Never once did a customer have to help herself: it was all weighed out, wrapped and passed over the counter. A bill was presented and was paid to the assistant, who gave the customer a receipt.

In those days, Woolworth's still sold everything for 6d (2p) or under. The counters were open, with one or two assistants standing in the well in the middle of four counters. One of the joys of life was wandering round Woolworth's to see what was happening, to meet friends and spend a little money on frivolities.

Alan Baker reflects on shop assistants then and now:
In recent years we have seen the demise of the small corner shop,

where one was always 'served' and where there was always the statutory chair, where customers could rest themselves, and get all their worries off their chests to a willing listener behind the counter. I am quite convinced that the 'small shopkeeper' was a sort of amateur psychiatrist – a listener who enabled many a customer to face another day without having to visit a doctor, social worker, probation officer or whatever! In short, shop work in the 1950s was very much what we now term a 'service industry' (a misnomer, I feel, when applied to a modern hypermarket!). In the 1950s it was still satisfying to please a customer, to iron out a dispute, to listen to a problem, to send the customer away pleased with the service they'd received. This applied whether in the one-man business or the branch of a large organisation. How different now, when shopping in a supermarket or self-service store is stressful enough, without the added indignity of passing through the checkout without a word from the overworked cashier.

Before the war, Daphne Stone's family had run a model-making business (display, architectural and theatrical) in Hythe. After the war they set up a business in a 'listed' building in the High Street:
My mother, a qualified needlewoman, attracted a large clientele of ladies, locally and from London, who, missing their West-End boutiques and seeking to use their clothing coupons to the best advantage, placed orders for bespoken, handmade lingerie, some from parachute silk brought home by ex-service members of the family.

At that time it was necessary to get a permit from the Chamber of Trade to start up in business, especially if one was considered new to the area, and likely to be competition with those who were gradually returning from wartime 'exile' or perhaps the forces. Today, shopping in the High Street, with these very same traders retiring one by one, it brings nostalgia to recall our first acquaintance with each other – young hopefuls getting married, starting families and so on. Among them was a loyal member of the 'Free Polish' who set up, after the war, as a tailor with a military touch!

6

CHILDREN

I will not go into cases. Still, standards were high, compared to today. Young ladies did not leave the house without wearing a hat and gloves, and always carried a clean handkerchief. They did not sit cross-legged.

Sylvia Hulme

Unlike today, when children frequently spend hours indoors watching TV or a video, in the 1950s the majority went out to play, as testified by many who wrote to us with happy memories of their childhood. Carol Williams remembers that 'We used to spend hours out in the fresh air' and Mrs F.E. Hamill recalls:

In the early 1950s there were hardly any cars about, and we could play in the streets. We played skipping, hopscotch, marbles, whip-and-top, hide-and-seek and lots of other games, without the worry of someone running away with us. When rationing ended, we used to run errands for neighbours who gave us pennies, and we'd go straight to René's for sweets. Saturday's sixpenny rush to the Apollo cinema on Berridge Road was great, and if you had a penny left afterwards, you went to a little shop and bought two Horlicks tablets and two ice-cubes.

My best friend was Ian Crowthall. We had a magical sort of communication with one another, quite beyond words. We planned to build a spaceship to go to the moon. We designed it on paper. It was to be built of a wooden orange-box with a gigantic gyroscope worked by a rope, which would then turn a huge propeller. I believe we even collected materials for making it.

Susan Cran

Valerie Heath also writes about playing outside:

None of us had very many toys, but there was plenty to do. Our parents and the local farmers were quite happy for us to roam the countryside all day, in a way that would be unthinkable now. Farms were smaller then, and they were mixed. On stock farms especially, there were more farm-workers in the fields, so I suppose we were not often out of an adult's sight. The hedges and fences were not as secure as they are now, either. Sheep and cows often escaped.

We played tiggy in fields where the buttercups whipped our legs, and sat down to make daisy-chains. We climbed trees and made a den in one huge hollow tree which held our most precious things in its hollow arms. We also had a 'house' in an old horse-drawn van that was no longer used. We paddled and played in the becks. One was wide, pebbly and full of watercress. The other was sandy and went through forbidding tunnels. We trapped fish in jam-jars in the first and made complicated dams in the other. We walked for miles north and south, but not so far east and west along the main road. Cars ran along this road to Scarborough. My parents didn't encourage me to play near it, as my grandfather had been the first person in the village to be killed by a car there. On Saturday we spent hours watching the cars pass, while each of us counted the cars of a particular colour. In those days, black always won.

We used to eat all sorts of wild plants and collect crab apples in the autumn. We made the plantains and cow-parsley stalks into harmless 'weapons'.

There were several disused limestone quarries, some old and grassed-over, two newer. They must have been used to build the houses in the village. Mounds of cowslips and harebells grew on the hillsides above the quarries, and when they flowered the air was scented. There were foxholes in the tree-roots round the quarries, and rabbits everywhere. They've all gone now.

In the 1950s people moved away from the centre of the village, and their houses became derelict. We used to play there, often helping the decay along by knocking the huge chalk stones out of their clay fixings. All the outside walls were double, with a gap of about eighteen inches between.

A lane ran along the bottom of our garden. On the other side of its hedge was a field that was never used for anything. It still had regular deep holes bored in it, to trap wartime invaders. The lane itself was narrow, and had thorn trees on both sides which met above. At Maytime I used to imagine I was in the White Way of Delight from *Anne of Green Gables*.

John Tyrrell also writes about how much fun he and his siblings used to have without lots of toys:
It is the house and garden I remember playing in most. They were enormous. My parents had begun their married life in a tiny terrace house in Glasgow (about which I remember nothing at all), but when I was seven, soon after the war, they had moved to a vast, semidetached mansion (as it seemed, and still seems, to me) on the outskirts of Bradford. How they afforded it I have no idea. It had been planned in much more spacious days. It was built on a hill, so that the front was one storey higher than the back. There were two huge cellars, one with a built-in stone table the size of a billiard table; a vast kitchen, scullery and quarry-tiled hall; two big sitting-rooms downstairs; three bedrooms and two bathrooms upstairs; four attics. Running round the eaves, linking the attics, was a 'secret' passage. I've no idea why it was built, but you could get into it through little doors in each attic, and terrify yourself to death.

I imagine that this house was built for families with servants, but it ideally suited our family of seven: two hard-working parents and five children. When we were young we used to play on the stairs and landing; we made a puppet theatre in one of the attics; we made tunnels and tree-houses in the garden. The house, being stone-built, was cool in summer and freezing cold in winter. I remember lying in my attic bedroom all one winter (I was about twelve), listening to a crystal set which a boy at school had made for me and reading books about Captain Scott's last expedition – an occupation for which the temperature, both outside and in, seemed just ideal.

Some of those who were children in the 1950s have still got their favourite toys somewhere. Maxine Elvey says: 'At the top of a wardrobe in my parents' house, there are two very large plastic bags full of toys from my childhood.' She continues:
Teddy bears and a rubber duck have long since disintegrated, but the plastic dolls, and their clothes, remain. When I was six I had the measles and could not go to my Uncle Fred's wedding. I spent the day at Nanna and Grampa's, and was given a large doll as compensation for not being able to go. I don't remember feeling ill, and thought I had a very good deal, being given such a wonderful doll. I called her 'Jennifer', I think because the old (as they seemed to

me) couple next door had a daughter called Jennifer, who used to play with me. When you turned Jennifer over, she said, 'Mamma', though it sounded more like 'Waa waa'! The sound came out of a voice box with holes on her back. She had jointed legs, so you could hold her and make her walk. She was called a 'Walkie-talkie' doll. Her blonde hair was in plaits: a fashion for some little girls in those days. Later, her wig got thin and matted, so we replaced it with another bought at Woolworth's, and stuck it on. In those days there were 'Dolls' Hospitals' for dolls that had got badly broken. Dolls sat on shelves in the windows, and inside were spare parts: heads, arms, legs, etc.

My second doll, nearly as big as Jennifer, was a model of Princess Anne (so her name was, of course, Anne). The Princess had pretty blonde curls in those days – and so did the doll. Later, other dolls were bought, including 'Topsy', a black plastic doll from Woolworth's. Dolls were purchased in pretty outfits, but you could buy packets of additional dolls' clothes in Woolworth's. Sometimes I spent my pocket-money on these. Like many things from Woolworth's in those days, they were cheaply made and tended to fall apart. Far better were the dolls' dresses lovingly sewn, knitted and crocheted by Mummy and Nanna: these still remain today.

In those days there were no safety regulations regarding toys, and soft toys had eyes on long pins that could be pulled out. My favourite toy, which still lives with me today, was 'Nicky', a corgi nightdress-case. My sister has 'Rusty', a cocker-spaniel nightdress-case, sitting on her bed. They were bought in about 1956 and were so well made that they are still going strong, though Rusty's fur is a little threadbare. However they, too, have eyes on long pins that can be pulled up and down.

Typical of a time in the 1950s, now collectors' pieces, were German clockwork toys. My sister had a monkey that rotated while beating a drum. I had a father mouse that while rotating, lifted a little girl mouse up and down. They were made of metal and dressed in felt. Both are in the toy bags on top of the wardrobe, and the monkey still works.

Not all families had money to spend on toys and dolls. For instance, many tried to make do with second-hand clothes, though not always with success, as Howard Palmer writes:

Once, my grandmother bought a brown gent's overcoat from a jumble sale, with the sole purpose in mind of having a small overcoat made out of it for me, as clothes were hard to come by. A friend of the family, a Mrs Holmes, made the overcoat and presented it to my mother. 'How lovely, it really fits him well', were her words to the woman as she tried the coat on me. I remember the coat was far too big and the bottom hem reached my ankles. After the woman left, my mother said I looked like Smike out of *Oliver Twist* in the coat and she wouldn't let me wear it. When my gran asked why I wasn't wearing the coat, as it was cold, my mother told her it didn't go with the red woollen pixie hat I wore in inclement weather.

Memories of cold weather are not all gloomy. Carol Williams remembers the excitement of celebrating winter festivals when she was young:

When the winter came, it was magical, as it brought Hallowe'en. My mother used to tie a piece of string across the room with apples attached to it, and we had to eat them with our hands tied behind our backs. Then we'd try to eat another apple, again with our hands out of the way, in a bowl of water. I still carry on this tradition with my own children, with a few witches, lanterns and ghost stories thrown in. They love it just as I did as a child and I love doing it for them.

Guy Fawkes Night was another magical time. My father used to buy a box of fireworks every year and light them in the front garden so that all the children in the street could enjoy them too. Then afterwards we all went to the field at the back of our house to light the bonfire which the boys had spent weeks preparing. The boys used to work hard collecting all sorts of things for it, and by the actual night it was quite large. Sometimes a group of boys from another area would mischievously light it a few weeks before – but we always knew, for our boys used to shout, 'The bonfire's on fire, the bonfire's on fire' and everyone ran to help put it out. Some of our boys would then make a den inside it to protect it – quite dangerous when you think of it. On the actual night, after the firework display and the bonfire had died down, we used to run home to get potatoes and then push them into the edge of the glowing embers with a stick. Most of the time they weren't cooked inside, but the taste was memorable nevertheless.

My parents weren't well-off, but they managed to make Christmas a happy time for my sister and me. I used to have the usual stocking filled with tangerines and nuts and some small presents, such as a colouring book, paints, soap, handkerchiefs etc. I was overjoyed. I remember one Christmas morning Dad asked me to get his slippers, which were in the corner of the room, and when I got there I found a beautiful dolls' house. He'd made it himself and had even put a little bulb in each of the rooms. I was really thrilled with that little house and used it for a long time. Another Christmas which I remember was the night that my friend and I went carol-singing and were asked into an elderly couple's house to sing. Afterwards they gave us some money and a mince pie each, and wished us a very happy Christmas! On our way home, all the street lighting was out due to a power failure – and when I got home I found my mother stuffing the turkey by candlelight. I remember thinking how Christmassy it was.

Maxine Elvey also recollects one Christmas in the 1950s:
When I was seven, and we were preparing for Christmas, I asked 'Mummy, how can Father Christmas go down all the chimneys of all the children in the world in one night?'. Mummy replied, 'It's really mummies and daddies who fill the stockings' – a revelation that I had not expected. That Christmas my sister Sylvia and I left our stockings on the tallboy outside the bedrooms instead of at the foot of our beds. Very early in the morning, when it was still dark, I got up in my long cotton nightie, and peered at the fascinating, bulging stockings. I walked into my parents' bedroom. My mother opened her bleary eyes. 'I've got a Muffin the Mule marionette, and Sylvia's got a Muffin glove-puppet,' I said excitedly. I knew that Mummy had bought them and put them there, but I still half-believed the Father Christmas fantasy, in the way that children merge fact and fiction in their minds.

While December brought the promise of Christmas celebrations, then as now winter was a time when children were more susceptible to illness. Elisabeth Brooke's account reveals how attitudes towards treatment and recovery have changed since the 1950s:
I see from my diary that on 19 January 1952 I felt sick, came home from school on Tuesday, went to bed with flu and stayed there until the end of the month, when I started getting up for longer and longer until I was up all day on Saturday 31 January. I had to be up for three days before I could go back to school on 3 February. This experience tells a lot about the treatment of childish ailments at that time. My mother was only a little more cautious than was usual. I was going to say 'than other mothers', but that is very much a phrase of today – there was no solidarity of mothers in the early 1950s in

our bit of East Yorkshire. Antibiotics were not prescribed as readily as they are today and were not, so far as I remember, particularly effective. Therefore illnesses ran their course, and there was a rehabilitation programme to be followed.

First you stayed in bed until your temperature had been down for a whole day. Then you were allowed up, in stages: for tea only; then for the whole afternoon but back in bed after tea; then for lunch and tea; then from mid-morning onwards (but early bed); then from breakfast onwards but early bed (because having been up all day you were thought to be exhausted). On the next day you were allowed outside for a bit; the following day for longer; and finally back to school. Today's laid-back assurance that the child will be all right in a day or two without antibiotics was absent. There was more caution and fear.

Gillian Bark also remembers being confined to bed:
In October 1954, at the age of seven, I was taken ill. What at first was thought to be a pulled muscle turned out to be polio. I was taken to Lincoln Hospital in an ambulance with my parents. I remember waking in the ambulance and seeing my mother (who was seven months pregnant) being sick into a basin, held by a nurse. Polio was confirmed next day, and I spent six weeks in hospital. Luckily I had a mild form of it. I was paralysed down my left side. There were three other children in the ward: a girl of about twelve, who had been in an iron lung from the age of four; another girl of about ten, and a boy of about five, who was later transferred to another hospital when it was discovered he had a tumour on his spine. The reason I don't give their names is that they all eventually died.

My parents visited me every Saturday afternoon, but were not allowed into the ward. They spoke to me through the french windows which led on to the verandah. At first I was flat on my back, then gradually raised on pillows, then one Saturday I was allowed to sit in a wheelchair for their visit. My mother hid herself and wept.

I recovered, learned to walk again with the aid of a doll's pram that had belonged to one of the dead children, and returned home. As a returning-home present, my teacher had bought me a doll and knitted it a full outfit of clothes in pale blue. My parents had also bought me a doll, which someone dressed as a bride at their request. (My father had bribed me to stop crying and go into hospital by saying that I could have anything I wanted on my return home.) The 'tallyman' (door-to-door salesman) we were friends with had brought me a doll's tea set, made of pot not plastic, and my younger brother Keith gave me six pink plastic doll-size teaspoons. All these presents were awaiting my return, arranged on the settee, on the day I came home. It was better than Christmas!

For weeks after I went back home, I had to have regular physiotherapy, and was taken to and from it in a hospital car. My mother attended pregnancy check-ups at the same time, and used to wheel me in a push-chair, with my brother Keith pedalling the three-wheeled bicycle that had once been mine. On 5 December I had a new baby brother, and in January I went back to school.

The way schools were run in the 1950s has left a strong impression on mothers and pupils alike. Often, schools had only one or two teachers giving all the lessons, as Rhoda Woodward describes:
My daughter started at the village school when she was five. There was only one teacher, from the five-year-olds to the elevens. She taught well, and had most of the children beginning to read after the first term. She had quite a good record for getting her pupils through their eleven-plus to go on to grammar school. She taught by the old-fashioned method of using the sound of the letters.

Rose Whittle adds:
In the 1950s my daughters went to the same school as I had, and in fact they had the same teacher. They loved their school and respected their teacher, and worked hard to learn. Parents all gave help and consideration to the teachers in those days.

Sheila Francis confirms that education was a serious business:
I was a primary school pupil in 1950. We had coal fires in the classrooms, and milk was warmed round the grate in bitter weather. Teachers were very strict, and each taught the class for one year. The teacher taught all types of things in the class: classical music, singing of well-known songs (ballad type, songs like 'Linden Lea' which would have been sung round the piano in times past), nature study and the three Rs, and would read the 'classics' to us. We learned a great deal.

She continues:
Talking in class earned you the cane, girls and boys alike, and the headmaster was the most feared man in the village. Today, he would

have been gaoled; but in those days he was held in the highest esteem and was respected. When you were sent to his room (which was quite rare), you really quaked in your shoes. He was about 60, short and stocky, and got into terrific rages when he would literally throw pupils across the room or drag them by the hair. He had a bamboo cane about ten feet long with which he could reach the class from his desk, and he certainly used it. No parents ever came to school to complain, and, of all the children in my class of at least forty, I don't know one who has gone wrong. The boys, now my age, have all done well. Two are now headmasters themselves, one has a large insurance company, and many others have good jobs.

I remember the first time school dinners came to our school, possibly in 1951. Our canteen was in a hall about 300 yards from the school, and each day, in all weathers, we paraded in a 'crocodile' there and back. I loved the dinners, they were delicious and nourishing.

In 1950, Valerie Heath was in her last year at the village school, which she remembers in detail:
There were three classrooms, and, at first, about ten classes. As the school leaving age went up, more of the top classes were sent to secondary schools each year. When I began at the school at the end of the war the oldest pupils were fifteen; when I left, the oldest pupils were thirteen.

The infants' classroom opened off the cloakroom. The next group of classes had to go through the big classroom to get to theirs. Most children wore hobnailed boots which made a loud, dull scraping along the wooden floor. Every time I have been into the school since, I have closed my eyes and heard it.

All three classrooms were heated by coal fires, stoked by the big boys (who did a great deal of manual work). Each fire had a huge guard with long bars, rather like a prison cell. It was very heavy and conducted heat from the fires in winter, so that it was a hazard in itself. In winter, the crates of bottled milk were put in front of the fires for about an hour to thaw.

The infants and girls shared one playground, and the boys had the other. Each playground had three bucket lavatories which stank, and had to be emptied. We had PT lessons – exercises, ball games and running games – in the playground; these were much more enjoyable than 'real' games.

The children kept their best dresses and suits for Sundays. You always went out for tea on Sunday. Apart from Sunday best they only had their school uniform and last year's Sunday best, no sports clothes or casual clothes like they have today.

The Coombes Croft Library Local History Group

As well as the usual school smells there was the smell of the ink, made from powder and water. It wasn't too unpleasant, just pervasive.

The head teacher and his wife taught the older classes and shared the big classroom. Mrs Newton's classes had their backs to the others; Mr Newton's were sideways on. Funnily enough, I can seldom remember being distracted by the other classes. But I was always aware of Lassie, the Newtons' dog. She was big, and her tail wagged a lot. Being short-sighted, I was at the front, and I used to tense, waiting for Lassie to turn away from me and lash my legs with her tail as she padded up and down the aisles. I didn't like big dogs.

Wartime paper-saving was still carried on. We learned, for example, to draw lines round each sum, and tried to fit as many as possible on each page – that was as important as getting them right.

In 1950 I passed my eleven-plus and went to grammar school. One of the first wonders I found there was the showers. Until then I'd always bathed in the same tub as I'd had as a baby. It leaked, had to be constantly filled up with water (specially heated as we only had one cold tap in the whole house), and the entire family used it. I never got over the thrill of constant, hot running water at school, and pirouetted as long as I could after gym lessons. I still remember that joy every time I have a shower now.

The cost of the school uniform was horrendous. As I lived in the East Riding of Yorkshire, and the school was in the North Riding, I was not eligible for the clothing grant. Until then, all my clothes were handmade, or hand-me-downs from better-off neighbours' nieces who lived in Glasgow. (Thank you, the Boyle family.) We managed to borrow a gymslip, which was in the St Trinian's style, not the proper uniform one. My mother made the blazer and my blouses. We had to buy the badge, tie, hat and sports shirts. The school had navy-blue knickers as regulation underwear and for gym and games. My knickers allowed so much room for growth that they came over my shoulders. I was about four feet five inches tall, and must have looked ridiculous. My vests stopped three inches above my waist. For hockey boots, my father nailed leather strips on to some second-hand shoes. One of our neighbours who worked in a leather shop in Scarborough produced a satchel that had been shop-damaged, and we got it at a huge discount. I set off in my haphazard collection of clothes, as proud as Punch, wearing huge, completely round NHS spectacles, and with my unruly hair crammed into thick plaits tied with navy-blue ribbons. For the first time ever, I was wearing white, not grey, ankle-socks on a weekday. It was heaven!

Colin Coupland remembers his secondary school, which was an old workhouse:
It was bleak, with small windows and dozens of tiny, four-inch squares of glass in each window. They were so old that the wind used to blow out many of these squares. It was a building quite similar to Buckingham Palace: you entered a courtyard through a big arch. The headmaster's study was on one side, and the main door of the school faced the entrance arch. There was a metal spiral staircase, leading up three storeys. There were also spiral staircases at each corner, with a door allowing entrance to each wing. There were no corridors. We had to pass through classrooms to reach the furthest ones – though this wasn't much of a disadvantage, because, apart from certain subjects such as woodwork, PE, games etc., we remained in the classrooms and the teachers came to us. I can remember Mr Mears the headmaster and Mr Thompson the deputy, both very strict. In fact, Mr Thompson had only to enter a classroom for there to be a deathly hush.

Outside school, pets featured in a number of children's lives, though on the whole fewer families owned them in those days, as Maxine Elvey writes:
In the 1950s many people had pets, but not nearly as many as today. When I visit my parents in London, as I walk down the road, the chances are that I will see three or four beautiful large cats sitting in front gardens. As a child, when I walked up and down the same road to and from school, I don't remember seeing any other cats except occasionally Fluffy, my cousins' cat at No. 13. I say 'other' because we had a grey tabby cat called Timmy Swops Bango Willy (Willy for short). My mother used to spend a lot of time cooking fresh food for Willy. She would get lights (lungs) from the butcher, and sprats, whiting and scraps (heads and tails) from the fishmonger. The kitchen constantly smelt of boiling fish – not pleasant. My cousin

Susan had a large brown tabby called Roly Poly. Before they had Fluffy, my cousins at No. 13 had a tortoise called Tammy, followed by a hamster called Hammy. We were friendly with one family who had eight cats – which seemed as unusual and eccentric as it would today. The cats used to go everywhere, and there were usually one or two asleep in a doll's pram.

Different breeds of dogs were fashionable in those days. Our next-door neighbours had a dog called Rover: I think it was a cross between a corgi and an alsatian (both popular breeds at the time). After Rover died they had a series of poodles, right up to their last dog, which must have died in the 1980s. In the 1950s, dachshunds, long and short-haired, were more common. My mother's cousin had one called Strudel, because his long shape resembled apple strudel. Another dog which was much more common then than today was the cocker spaniel, either golden or black and white. My mother's relation Rose had one that smelt of stale biscuits. I'm sure that much about social attitudes can be judged by breeds of dogs popular at any particular time.

Maxine Elvey also remembers how she received her sex education:
When I was six I had the measles, and as I lay in bed I asked my mother a lot of questions. One was, 'How does the baby get inside the mummy's tummy?' My mother told me, and was always proud of her broad-mindedness, telling me at such a young age. I thought it was rather bizarre, and it sat at the back of my mind for years.

Sex was not talked about in primary schools, at least not in middle-class Southgate. When I was in the fourth year at Osidge Junior School, I sat next to a girl called Susan Whitehead, at one of the double desks we used to have. We must have started talking about babies, and she said, 'I wonder how the seed from the man gets to the egg in the woman'. The fact that had lain in the back of my mind for so long was remembered. I said, 'The man puts his thing in her thing'. Susan said that she didn't believe me. However, the next day she said, 'You're right. I asked my mother. My mother said, "Have the girls at school been saying anything?" and I said "No". So she told me.'

In the same year, the fourth year of junior school, Mrs Cunningham, our class teacher, gave the girls a special talk. All the boys were sent out, and the girls from the other fourth-year class (we were 'birthrate bulge' children, so there were a lot of us) came to join us. In a very fruity voice Mrs Cunningham announced, 'I'm going to talk to you about your monthly periods. How many of your mothers have discussed them with you?' A minority, perhaps a third, put our hands up. I don't remember any of the girls having periods at that age (about ten years old). If they did, it would have been the odd one or two, and they probably kept it secret. Puberty generally came later then than it does today.

In the first year of my secondary school, a group of girls sat on desktops one lunch hour, discussing the fact that the mother of one of us was pregnant. I said that periods stopped during pregnancy. The others said that this was nonsense, but the next day the girl whose mother was pregnant confirmed the fact. So at that age, eleven and twelve, we can have had no accurate knowledge about why women have periods. Sex education at East Barnet Grammar School consisted only of human reproduction as part of the O Level course in the fourth year. However, as we were teenagers, sex was discussed a lot and some started experimenting with it from the age of about fifteen. But of course, by then we were into the 1960s.

At home, a favourite hobby for many children was reading. Elisabeth Brooke writes:
I see from my 1952 diary that on 1 January I wrote to Lorna Hill, whose 'Sadlers Wells' stories are still in print today. A reply came on 13 January, telling me that she was writing two books. Round that date in my diary I put 'Day of my Life', and at the end of the entry 'I can't get over thinking about the letter'. On 3 September 1952 I wrote to Malcolm Saville (another children's author still in print in 1992), and had a reply on 8 September. I was at the time reading his *Secret of the Hidden Pool*, and was rationing myself to one chapter a day so that it would last. Books were very important to me, and I loved reading more than anything. Whatever else I read in 1952, base stock was the *Anne of Green Gables* series (by L.M. Montgomery), Louisa M. Alcott's *Little Woman*, the Katy books, D.F. Bruce's Dimsie books (school stories), all Malcolm Saville and Lorna Hill.

Valerie Heath was also a voracious reader:
I went to a village primary school, and the tiny 'library' was suitable for much older chidren and adults. In any case, we weren't allowed to borrow from it until we were in the top class. As a family, we couldn't afford to buy books as a rule, but my mother saved hard to get us hardback books for birthdays and Christmas. She collected for me the *Anne of Green Gables* series, which I read so many times I

could chant parts from memory. Each year, I used to get another, unexpected, book for attendance at Sunday School. I loved *Tom Sawyer* and *Ivanhoe*, hated *Vanity Fair* and *The Bluestocking Ladies*. When I went to grammar school I just couldn't believe my luck. Shelves and shelves of books that we were *encouraged* to read! We were allowed to take two fiction books each day, and I did that almost every school day until I was fifteen. My mother and I were both compulsive readers, and we read them all. We started with the girls' boarding-school stories (how incredibly unlike our own lives!), and moved on eventually to the classics. After three years I started at letter A and read all the books I'd missed.

As money became a little easier in the 1950s, we began a complex system of swapping bought books, library books and magazines with some of our (female) relations. One of my aunties belonged to the Companion Book Club, another to Boots Lending Library.

But for all young people, readers or not, times were about to change.
Sheila Francis remembers:
Sunday evening in about 1955 or 1956, while listening to Radio Luxembourg on the new-fangled 'portable' radio, a sound was heard and the world was never the same again. Suddenly ELVIS PRESLEY sang 'Heartbreak Hotel', and the songs we'd known before became ghosts from another era.

Ms Kay Wilson remembers another phenomenon of the time – very popular when not all teenagers yet had gramophones or cassette-players of their own:
As adolescents, we would go to the record shop, to listen to 78s of the latest 'pop', wearing our flat shoes and circular, decorated-felt skirts and yards of net underskirt. The listening-booths were at the back of the ancient shop, and the floors were of bare earth.

Things were improving on the fashion scene as well – as Anne Filkin remembers:
I was a young woman when clothes were rationed so I hailed the end of that with even more glee. No more cutting up parachutes to make undies, or unpicking jumpers. At school I'd worn boys' shoes which cost only three coupons, instead of five. We had it all worked out. But we longed for lots of pretty clothes. And they *were* pretty; I feel a bit sad that girls nowadays seem obliged to look grim.

Maureen Weitman echoes these sentiments:
To be young in the 50s was a bonus. Beautiful models like Barbara
Goalen introduced us to the latest fashion. Pristine appearance was
every girl's aim: we wanted to look immaculate, coiffeured heads held
high. It was an era of stiletto heels, flounced skirts, nipped-in
'waspie-waists', seamed stockings and white cotton gloves. By the
mid-1950s duffel coats had made an appearance, along with coffee
bars and the reincarnation of the 1940s', 'Bohemian' style.

*Fashion, of a rather more flamboyant kind, was very much on Sheila
Francis' mind:*
The mid-1950s saw the emergence of 'Teddy boys' and 'Teddy girls',
and in my Welsh village I was in the forefront. Remember, there
were no fashions in those days: young people were too afraid of
public opinion. I managed to buy a black coat and trousers in a
jumble sale, and my bootlace tie *was* a bootlace. Clothes were
sneaked out, and you dressed in a secluded place near the bus stop.

Jane Fraser Cross remembers two other popular teenage activities:
My hobby was tap-dancing and singing, and I loved the Saturday-
night hop. Public houses were out of bounds to me, so it was the
coffee bars where we met our boyfriends. A cup of coffee cost us
practically nothing.

*In many parts of the country, a favourite way of meeting the opposite
sex was 'Monkey Parades'. Sheila Francis explains how the system
worked in her area of Wales:*
'Monkey Parades' took place on Sunday evenings, and young people
would walk round a specific area mostly in a clockwise direction – it
was rare to go round the other way. The walks took place in summer
and winter, but winter was much more exciting. Lighting was only
from streetlamps, shops were not lit then; the exciting part came
when you met someone and didn't exactly know what he/she looked
like.
    People would gather around 7pm, usually about three or four girls,
sometimes two, same for boys. Many would go to church or chapel
first, the walk would begin and people would look at each other.
Perhaps you would pass them for an hour before anything was said.
If each party liked what they saw, they would follow the other
person, or call them to talk next time round. This went on until
about 9–9.30pm (youngsters then had to be in at 10pm at the very

latest, even boys, and many had a bus to catch to outlying areas.) If the weather was wet or very cold, with thick frost, people went into the many Italian cafés which abounded in that small area. This was the start of the coffee bar culture which came much later. One cup of froth and out you went again.

When you met a boy you liked, he took you to your bus or walked you home, even if you lived twenty minutes' walk away. A date was fixed, usually for the coming Saturday, and to the 'pictures' of course. The local cinema had expensive seats – 2/11d (15p) – and if you were seen in these you were 'somebody'. The boys ALWAYS paid for the girl, the girl never paid half, it wasn't done, and you were usually bought a box of chocolates too. When the film ended he saw you home or to your bus. If you didn't 'hit it off', you didn't turn up on your next date but went back on the walk again.

Many girls met their future husbands in these parades. The average age of the walkers would be around fourteen to sixteen. Parades also went on in Swansea (where people walked along the Prom) and in a town five miles away. If you went there you were very daring.

7

THE FESTIVAL OF BRITAIN

Britain Can Make It!
Government slogan

The Festival of Britain was held in 1951, 100 years after the Great Exhibition which had celebrated the wonders of the Victorian Age. It was part of the government's plan to bring some cheer into everyone's grim post-war lives. Its purpose was to show the glories of Britain: our skills in the arts and sciences, our developments in architecture, town planning and technology since the war – our becoming, in fact, a streamlined, modern nation.

The site for the Festival, a bombed-out area south of Vauxhall Bridge on the Thames in London, was cleared and laid out with gardens, pavilions, walks and public buildings. Further along were fun-fairs, boating lakes and roller-skating rinks. Nothing like it had been seen in Britain for years, and visitors poured into London in their millions. The ladies from the Coombes Croft Library Local History Group remember:

We had to go several times, whenever we had visitors. They wanted to see everything, because they wouldn't get another chance. We were always exhausted when we got back home, because it was such a big site to walk round. You didn't want to miss anything. We'd had nothing all during the war, and at the start of the 1950s it was great.

One member of the group, Mrs Leonie Kitchener, recalls a particular wonder: the Guinness clock which had 'doors that opened, figures that moved and all sorts of chimes and tunes and noises' when it struck the hour, to the delight of watching crowds.

The Festival was fun for adults, but for children it was Wonderland. Howard Palmer, then a child of about seven, says:

I remember the Skylon and the Dome of Discovery. Dad said, as we looked up at the Skylon, if it collapsed and fell in our direction we'd all be killed. I pulled him away quickly, saying I wanted a toffee apple. The sight of the sculptured lions and unicorns against a wall filled me with awe because of their size. Later in life, as an adult, I saw them again, in the Festival Gardens, and was amazed how small they were.

During the day my father bought me a topee. I'd seen them being sold by a man on a stall, and I kept worrying my father until he got me one. My gran used to take me to the cinema and we had seen several Tarzan films and films set in Africa. All the 'good guys' wore pith helmets so I wanted one. In any case such a hat would afford me good protection in the event of the Skylon falling on me. I must have looked a sight as the helmet swamped my head, even though it was the smallest size.

On the way home the coach stopped at a pub so that the passengers could relieve and refresh themselves. The men bought crates of beer on to the bus and everyone was drinking. I had a soft drink and a packet of crisps. Presently, they all started singing and one of the songs was 'Roll out the Barrel'. Whenever I hear that song now, it reminds me of the Festival of Britain.

Valerie Heath, on a school trip from Yorkshire, was slightly older – but her sense of wonder was much the same:
The two Scarborough grammar schools hired a train between them, but boys and girls were kept separate. As with all school parties, one of the greatest adventures was the journey. Once in London, I remember very little with any clarity. But there was the Skylon, the Dome of Discovery and – I think – a self-powering, endlessly nodding line of metal birds dipping their heads into water. I *do* remember boys supposedly playing a machine – a computer – at chess. The machine was surrounded by huge boxes like wardrobes. Everybody claimed that the machine really was playing, but I thought that they were stupid. Any fool could see that there was enough room for several Grand Masters to be hidden away in the wardrobes. The other thing I remember are the cups which had to be thrown away, because they were plastic. Throwing away anything, particularly something as useful as a cup, was to me like a mortal sin. London was clearly a place whose values were different from those of the Yorkshire Wolds, and I resolved to live there when I grew up, so that I, too, could be decadent.

8

FLOODS

The houses just fell over backwards into the river.

Roy Floyd

In the 1950s, Frank Goldsworthy was a news reporter on the Daily Express. *His* Memoirs *include this account of the disastrous floods in Devon in 1952 and on the East Coast in 1953:*

In some ways I rather enjoyed weather stories – taking a turn at oars in boats rescuing stranded householders, struggling through drifts to reach a snowed-in train or creeping through dense fog to a railway collision. All presented physical challenges. In those days I regarded thigh boots and wellingtons as standard equipment to be carried in the car boot, like a bag of coins for telephone boxes.

But Lynmouth in 1952 and the East Coast in 1953 were different: they were killers.

It was tea time on an August Saturday, my day off, when Tom Wilson rang from the *Express* newsroom to ask me to leave at once for Lynmouth in Devon. Some 180 rain-swept miles later I reached the point where a bridge marked the entrance to the town. Or had done. All that could be seen in the dark was a white creaming torrent over a jumble of boulders with wrecked cars jammed among them. Nine inches of rain – a quarter of the annual average – had fallen on Exmoor in a few hours on Friday night. This, coupled with the collapse of a moorland reservoir, had so swollen the twin rivers, East and West Lyn, that they joined to smash down houses, carry away 60 cars and a bus, and drown thirty-one people.

There was nothing to do but retreat to the Porlock Hotel, to spend the night and meet my Bristol colleague Jim Brady. Next morning, so many bridges were down that I had to drive over 80 miles round Exmoor just to reach the other side of that same swept-away bridge. On the last mile, driving down the valley road from Barbrook into

Lynmouth, I came to two garden gates with 'Bed and Breakfast' signs swinging in the wind. Behind them was a steep muddy slope to the swollen river. They marked the spot where Nos. 9 and 10 Barbrook Road had stood till the river scooped away their foundations and then devoured them. Of 11 and 12 not even the garden gates survived.

Over a wooden trestle table in a refugee centre, Tom Floyd and the surviving members of his family pieced together for me the tragedy of Nos. 9, 10, 11 and 12 Barbrook Road. They had been stone-built council houses with neat back gardens overlooking the West Lyn twenty feet below. Nos. 9, 11 and 12 had all been occupied by various units of the Floyd family. Tom and his wife Mary lived at No. 11 with their son, their daughter, her husband and their two grandchildren. They had two bed-and-breakfast guests from County Durham. The West Lyn drowned all these people except Tom.

In No. 12 had lived Tom's married daughter, her husband and three sons. When the storm hit the Lyn Valley, the parents were out and the boys were on their own. No. 12 took the full force of the torrent and as the house began to crack and water poured into the front door, the oldest boy Roy (sixteen) climbed out of the window and with two-year-old John in his arms waded chest-deep across the road, now a torrent, and climbed a bank, where his middle brother joined him. Roy told me, 'I saw Granpa come to his front door at No. 11. Granma and Uncle Fred were with him. As they stood in the doorway the two houses just fell over backwards into the river.'

Tom owed his life to the fact that his other married daughter, from No. 9, had already left her cracking house with her husband and daughters, and had reached the safety of the bank on the other side of the flooded road. Tom had grabbed at some heavy masonry and pulled himself on to the bank, only to be swept off his feet again by the water pouring down the road. His daughter had leaned out, seized her father's braces and swung him on to the bank.

Tom's daughter also said that Mrs Ridd, who lived at No. 10 with her eight-year-old grandson, had been in earlier in the evening to say that she had two girl hitch-hikers staying with them for the night. But the house had collapsed into the river, and none of them were ever seen again.

The story of what happened to the people of Nos. 9, 10, 11 and 12 Barbrook Road, and all the other stories and statistics gathered by my reporter colleagues, touched the nation's heart. Within days £300,000 had been subscribed to a relief fund, and 180,000 parcels of clothing arrived like a deluge of goodwill. Indeed, it was one of the few occasions when relief material exceeded the need – and some of it was used to help victims of an even bigger disaster, the East Coast floods, which struck just five and a half months later.

The East Coast floods happened on the night of 31 January 1953. They were caused by gale-force winds (over 160km/h, some of the highest ever recorded in Britain) combined with an abnormally high spring tide. Waves surged along the whole East Coast, from the Orkneys to the Thames estuary, causing devastation and disaster. Mr Goldsworthy's Memoirs *continue:*

I remember that on the evening of 31 January, my wife and I had been to a presentation of radio awards, and as we drove home the wind had brought an exceptional clarity to the lights of London. That same wind was driving an unprecedented sea-surge against the East Coast defences. By Monday morning the headline was 152 *KNOWN* DEAD. That was an understatement: the figure was eventually doubled. And across the North Sea in Holland, 1800 people died.

That Sunday morning reporters were being despatched in all directions. One went to record the evacuation of 10,000 people from Canvey Island. Another was in the Norman church at Great Wakering, talking to people who had spent the bitterly cold night on the roofs of their flooded homes. Another, on the edge of the cut-off Isle of Sheppey, found a bus whose twenty-eight passengers had spent the night sitting on the backs of the seats with water almost up to their knees. Still another had gone to meet 6,000 people evacuated from Mablethorpe and Sutton-on-Sea after the sea wall collapsed.

My own assignment was the below-sea-level village of Jaywick, near Clacton-on-Sea, where 600 people huddled on rooftops or sun balconies, or in lofts, waiting for volunteers in small boats to rescue them. The sea had smashed through the sea wall and swept across the marshes to invade Jaywick Hollow at 2am, the noise of its approach masked by the howling of the gale. The bungalow dwellers woke to find water up to bed level. They reached for the light but the electricity had gone. So had the telephones. The water was too deep to wade to higher land. So, still in their night clothes, they had climbed to roofs or lofts, there to endure the bitter cold. Next morning some of them were dead.

I went out by boat that day and later, searching for survivors. We found them blue and almost unconscious, and ferried them to waiting ambulances. With the people came their cats and dogs; unnumbered farm animals died.

P.E. Corbett remembers the floods on Canvey Island:
We had a dinghy in our garden at the time, and it came in very useful. As the sirens woke us up that night, we grabbed coats over our night attire. It was bitterly cold. As we made it to the front gate, we could see a torrent of water rushing along the road. Our bungalow was higher than the road, fortunately, so my husband had time to pull the dinghy into the water, and we rowed down the road to our neighbour's three-storey house, and were able to go to the top floor for the rest of the night.

Joan Harper and her husband were living on the Essex marshes, not far from Tilbury. On the morning after the flood, Mr Harper set off for work on his bike as usual. Joan Harper continues:
When he looked round, all he could see for miles was water, and he stupidly thought, 'It must have rained last night'. He carried on, but there was so much water that he came home to get his wellington boots and to tell me about it. Then, growing more and more certain that something was very wrong, he rode to the outskirts of Tilbury. People were looking out from their upstairs windows, and by now the water had reached the crossbar of his bicycle. He decided to call it a day. He phoned me and told me that water was lapping the phone in the box.

My husband found out afterwards that if he had ridden along the railway track he would have got to work – except that at one point the track was washed away and an engine had come to grief, rearing in the air like some monster. People from Tilbury had to be evacuated to higher ground (Chadwell St Mary), which was no mean feat. Many factories in the Purfleet area suffered a great deal of damage. The Thames Board Mills, which manufactured huge reels of paper, were in this area, and the reels were strewn round the countryside as if some giant had been throwing them in all directions.

We had visits from the Queen Mother, Princess Margaret and the Queen, which cheered people along. The floods at last subsided, and life slowly got back to normal – though things were not so easy for some of the poor souls whose homes had been ruined.

In another part of her letter, Mrs Harper mentions the help given by some US airmen stationed here. RAF personnel also gave sterling service. On the night of the floods, Geoffrey W. Shardlow and a coach party of fellow airmen were guests at a navy dance in Chatham. In the late evening the dance was stopped, and everyone was ordered to return to base. When the RAF coach reached the Medway, it was halted by the floods. Geoffrey Shardlow continues:

We took the exhaust manifold off the engine and then, fumes filling the bus, we drove safely to the other side, the last vehicle to pass for many days. Entering camp at 6am, we found a flurry of furious activity: our men were going to the Essex coast where the sea defences had been breached and some of the most serious flooding had happened. Later that day, our coach 'party' joined them in Canvey Island, with its storm-damaged buildings, flood-water and debris everywhere, and the dead some on rooftops, some in trees. It was the first time I'd ever seen a dead person. We travelled around in rowing boats, rescuing the living from rooftops, the dead from the murky water, then filling and stacking sandbags to try and secure the sea defences. After three days and nights we returned to our station. I slept for thirty hours – the only time I've ever slept all through a day.

Robin Ollington gives a vivid description of the night of the floods much further north, in Lowestoft:

It all began with a telephone call. My in-laws had gone to an Annual Dinner Dance at the Royal Hotel on the seafront, leaving myself, my wife and my young brother-in-law at home. During the course of the evening, my brother-in-law answered the telephone, and came rushing through with the news that his mother had phoned from the hotel to say that it was being flooded and would we leave immediately to collect her 80-year-old mother from her house before the floods arrived.

Knowing my brother-in-law, we took this message with something of a pinch of sea salt. I telephoned the hotel to check whether it was true. To my surprise I was informed that the sea had indeed come over the promenade, that it appeared to be still rising and that all the guests were upstairs. We set off down the main street towards the harbour to rescue Grandma. Other people were heading in the same direction. When we reached Station Square, facing the harbour, we found to our amazement that it was covered in water, with waves beginning to lap against the shop-fronts. In the darkness we could make out the shapes of ships in the harbour, looming much higher than usual above the quayside.

At this point the sea reached the town power supply, and suddenly everything was plunged into darkness, making the scene even more sinister and bizarre. We made off in the direction of Grandma's house. It proved impossible: whichever street we took, we found waves creeping insidiously along the gardens towards us in the dark, barring our way. We finally reached her house by a roundabout route, and found her still dry, but in total darkness and (because there was no power for radio or TV) totally unaware of what was happening. My wife persuaded her to retreat upstairs, and we piled furniture on tables ready for when the water came. (As it turned out, fortunately, it never did.)

When everything seemed ready, I borrowed some waders and left the house to rescue, or find out what had happened to, other in-laws. Walking eventually turned into wading. At one point in the darkness I came across a fellow-traveller who, like me, was feeling his way along the walls. As we approached Bevan Street and the shops, we had to dodge packing-cases and barrels which had gone afloat from the shops and cellars beneath them, and were bobbing around, banging into shop doors and windows.

Suddenly to my amazement, my companion vanished. He had plunged into a cellar whose flaps had opened with the water. Fortunately he rose to the surface fairly quickly and I grabbed him by the neck and pulled him up. Then, soaking, we continued on our way. Station Square was in total darkness. There were a few stranded cars, and a lone figure sitting on top of a phone box in the middle.

My way to the Royal Hotel led me over the Swing Bridge. As this was higher than the surrounding ground, it had become a haven for stranded people trying to get from North to South Lowestoft or vice versa. They were being piggy-backed to the higher levels nearby, or into the railway station which (also being higher) had become a collecting point.

When I reached the hotel, I wandered the candle-lit rooms upstairs and eventually discovered that my in-laws had managed to get on one of the Corporation buses which, because they were diesel-powered, had been able to run in the water much longer than conventional petrol-powered vehicles. I heard that patrons of the Palace Cinema nearby had been somewhat surprised to discover themselves ankle-deep in water, as the sea came in through the back doors; at St John's Church children holding a party in the hall had to seek refuge, so it was said, on the church altar and be rescued by boat!

I went back to the Swing Bridge, and helped piggy-back quite a few of the stranded people to the station, where fires were by now burning to keep people warm. By this time various rescue services were being swung into action. I remember that down in the Beach Village (which was behind the sea wall and so the worst-affected area) there was an act of considerable heroism: one of the men at the Gas Works stayed at great personal risk to rake out the furnaces, thus avoiding what could have been a huge explosion. I think that he was later awarded a medal for his bravery.

The next day, ironically, dawned bright and sunny. It was possible to see the outcome of the night before. Down in the Beach Village people were trapped upstairs in their houses, while the publicity slogan for Lowestoft, 'Where Broadland Meets The Sea', had become an awful reality as the waters of Lake Lothing on the sea side had swept across the road at Oulton Broad and joined up with the Broad, passing through shops and buildings *en route*.

My mother was Centre Organiser for the WRVS, and was immediately involved in setting up shelters in local church halls and organising supplies of clothes, blankets and food. I went off to the beach in a fire-engine to help collect the stranded, and we found people – and even, in one house, a pony – hanging out of bedroom windows. One pub in the harbour area had been flooded, with the result that the customers stayed all night, celebrating their good fortune.

St Margaret's Church Hall was pressed into use for homeless families and my wife and I went to help look after the children (who of course were treating the whole thing as a marvellous excuse for fun). The army came to join the helpers, complete with cooks and stoves, and the RAF produced large drying-units to help dry out the houses. No gas was available for some time, though electricity was restored after a few days. Everybody learned to improvise: I remember kitchens busy with Primus stoves, oil stoves, paraffin lamps and so on. When the gas was finally restored, people were warned not to turn it on or light it until a qualified fitter had called and checked it. To this end, gasmen were drafted in from all over the country. They went from house to house and ticked each house by the front door with chalk as it was cleared. However, the day was punctuated by the odd explosion as impatient householders tried to do it themselves and blew out their windows.

Needless to say, flood-damage sales were much in evidence for months afterwards and many people were able to buy bargains.

Down on the beach the houses were badly water-damaged, and it took a long time for them to dry out and be repaired. In the course of later redevelopment, this once lively and historic area became an industrial estate, and all traces of the floods have now virtually vanished except in the memories of people still living.

Robin Ollington adds a wry point – not about Frank Goldsworthy and the Daily Express *but about some of his less scrupulous reporter-colleagues:*
In the days following the floods, the national press had a field day. Lowestoft was full of reporters – and what we saw in the press was sometimes far from reality. One picture I remember in a paper showed some huge treetrunks which had been stored down on the beach for a timberyard, had worked loose during the flood and floated around. The press caption read, 'Giant trees uprooted by the storm'. I also remember a picture of a local vicar being carried to his church by a fireman. The water was in fact only nine inches deep, and both were wearing wellingtons – so why the need for carrying?

In fact, as Frank Goldsworthy's reports show, there was no need for such flamboyant invention. Reality was extraordinary enough, terrible enough. Mrs F.E. Hamill tells of a local butcher who kept a caravan at Skegness – until the floods, when it was washed much further along the coast, to Mablethorpe, about twelve miles away. Irene Pugh remembers her mother going to help her flooded brother and sister on Canvey Island, and being so affected by the stench in the bungalow that she had to run outside to vomit. Colin Coupland remembers the hotel at Sutton-on-Sea, which had completely lost one side wall, leaving all its rooms exposed. He goes on:
Friends of mine helped to clear up people's houses, and brought back some horrific stories. Mud and sand were everywhere, even inside ovens and cupboards. Some ovens still contained meals. They said that as they travelled in, they could see seaweed, straw and grasses hanging from telephone wires and trees as far as ten miles inland.

Leslie Blowers describes the painful process of getting back to normal after the floods devastated a small engineering factory in Colchester:
The factory had been under about three feet of water. On opening the doors we were faced with utter devastation. To make the situation worse, a large metal tank containing varnish had overturned, spilling its contents over the dirty flood water so that all

the machines were covered with sticky varnish and filth. It took three days of intensive effort by a very willing and enthusiastic work-force using water and solvents to clear up before we could attempt limited work again. Then we were further held up my the mains blowing: this caused at least another 24 hours' delay. Several of our slow payers rallied immediately, settling their debts in order to keep the firm going. But it was many weeks before we were in full production again.

Mrs J.K. Hawkins of Bradwell remembers a similar agonising process of clearing up, this time at home – and her story, at least, has a happy ending:
One friend took our carpets and hosed them down and dried them out. Another lady let us have her bungalow for a fortnight while we got cleaned up. Although the water ran out as soon as the tide turned, it left an awful lot of mud and rubbish behind. To quote one old neighbour, 'I opened my door and in came a bloody great turnip!' We came back home to bare boards and hard wooden chairs. We couldn't put anything on the floors for a long time, and we had to have the walls replastered to stop the rising damp. Eventually we got a home together again. I am now 79, still living in the same cottage, and there is no sign of damp anywhere. But it was an experience I wouldn't want to go through again.

9

Work

We had good laughs, more than we can today.
                                            Rose Whittle

During most of the 1950s, the school leaving-age was fifteen. Some of those who left school went on to further training, for example college courses and apprenticeships. Others started employment as 'juniors', very much on the bottom rung of the ladder of wages and status. Others again were plunged, almost from the first day, into full-scale, adult jobs. In mining or metal-working areas, such jobs could be physically tough, as Sheila Francis describes:

There were plenty of jobs: we could pick and choose. But all the work was hard. Three shifts were worked, 6am–2pm, 2pm–10pm and 10pm–6am. Loud hooters sounded at 1pm, 4.30pm and 10pm; everyone knew the time by that. You were expected to put in a full day's effort. The steel and tinworks were hot from the furnaces, you breathed thick gases and fumes, and the work was strenuous. (I expect the colliery was worse.) You gave all, or almost all, your wages to your parents.

Girls had less choice in deciding what jobs to do than boys. Janet Johnston remembers:

As my father wasn't keen for me to go on to further education, I began looking for a job. The choice seemed to be office, factory or shop-work – and as I didn't want to work in a factory or shop, the office it had to be! I was fortunate that a firm of accountants and auditors wanted someone to take over the office duties when the present person left to have a baby. I'd been attending night school for typing during the previous year. After an interview at the firm I was accepted. It was arranged that I should go in for a few Saturday mornings to learn the ropes. I was paid 2/6d (12½p) per Saturday.

When I started full-time work, my wages were £2-10s-0d (£2.50) per week. The firm was small, with only two partners. I was the only person in the office to answer the telephone, type accounts, audit and make the tea. I worked for this firm until I married and moved out of the area.

Sylvia Hulme was brought up in a children's home, and describes how care continued when she left school at sixteen and began her first job:
In 1953 I went to live in a hostel for young working women. I had a job near by in a brand new small factory. Nylon stockings were just coming in as an alternative to silk or lisle, and the Bear Brand Factory had just opened. As soon as I got my first wage packet, I handed it to our housemother: £3-10s-6d (£3.52½).

In the hostel, there were four rooms, each with twelve girls in it: Pink Room, Blue Room, Green Room, Yellow Room. Just as in the children's home, the residents did the chores on a rota basis, before and after work. The money we gave the housemother was divided up as follows: £2 for board and lodging, 10/- (50p) saved for clothes, 10/- (50p) saved for holidays, 8/- (40p) post office savings, and 2/6d (12½p) to spend. We used to go to the church Youth Club on Thursday evenings, and if we wanted to go to the cinema on Saturday evenings, our money would only stretch to one visit to the village milk bar.

Peter Poole struggled for a time on even less money – and also found it hard to find work that suited him:
A few months after I left school, I began working as an assistant to the golf professional at Churston golf course, between Brixham and Paignton. My pay was £1-10s-0d (£1.50) and I had to work six and a half days each week for this princely sum, the idea being that I was being taught to play golf on a professional basis, and also how to make and repair golf clubs.

It was soon apparent, however, that I had no aptitude whatsoever for playing golf, and my efforts were utilised on the repair side. After a year I left to begin my second job as a radio and television salesman (junior dogsbody), at three times the pay received at the golf course. After one year at this, I enlisted for four years in the RAF.

In those days of comparatively full employment, many young people simply took the first job that came along. They knew that, as Pat Wilson says,

. . . if you didn't like it, you could just go and get another. There was no problem. Every child left school with a job to go to, and women could find part-time work anywhere if they wanted it: firms were glad to have them on any terms.

Much of the work offered to young people or part-timers was very poorly paid – one reason why there was such flexibility about people moving from job to job. For older people, with families and heavier commitments, it could be more of a problem finding work that paid a 'living wage'. Mr E.H. began his working life as a baker, and worked at it for several years until the job simply collapsed under him, and his search for work began:

In May 1953 my boss closed his bakery business and we were all out of work – seven of us: bakers, roundsmen, confectioners, shop assistants. We all had one week's wages and then we were on our own. I had a mortgage of £33-6s-8d (£33.33) every six months, plus interest (two-and-three-quarters per cent). Wages at the bakery had been 2/5d (12p) an hour: one old penny over the union rate. I had worked forty-eight hours per week, including a little overtime and nightwork, and my average weekly wages had been about £7-5s-0d (£7.25). Of course money went further then: a two-pound loaf of bread cost 4½d (under 2p), and a small loaf cost 2½d (just over 1p).

In our area, work was in short supply that May. I passed over the Labour Exchange, and made enquiries myself for various trades including GPO telephones, builders, electric light and the local council. The council offered me a job as refuse-lorry loader (dustman): wage £6-10s-0d (£6.50) per week. If anybody says anything about dustmen, I say, 'Put a pair of overalls on and go out and do the job'. Surprisingly, I learned quite a few things, especially my way round the district. On Fridays we usually travelled 65 miles.

In most trades and professions, working conditions have completely changed since the 1950s. As Jean Gostelow sharply remarks, 'Fewer hours, health and safety rules, factory inspections – compared to us, people today don't know they're born'. Working conditions in some heavy industries, in particular, were very little different in the 1950s from a century before. Catherine Burns describes working as a dyer at the Paisley Anchor Works – a job she began in the war, when all the men were away fighting, and continued right through the 1950s:

We started at 6am: we had to leave home just after 5am to get to work in time. My first impression of my job was horror, as we had to wear clogs on our feet, masks over our mouths, and big dungarees to keep the water out. We never got any days off, and even worked on Christmas Day and Saturday. The work was very heavy, and we never got a minute to ourselves.

Sheila Francis tells a horrifying tale of the dangers lurking round another industrial plant:
When I was about ten or eleven, after Sunday school, I was sent to the large tin works, a few minutes' walk away, with Dad's tea in a basket. Dad worked a special shift some Sundays, when he would be the only worker there. (There was a watchman, but he was at the gate office.) The large works' gate had a small door set in it. I used to go in, and tell the watchman where I was going; he waved me through, and after a short walk I entered the work area, which was vast. There were fires under the stone floor, down steps, and Dad's job was to attend to them all, thus keeping fluid the molten tin on top. Machinery was everywhere, and I would ride on a swing-like gantry. While Dad ate his meal or did his work I used to wander all round the works. In the adjoining area was a room which I now shudder to think of. Four huge vats were sunk into the floor, not cordoned off; they were full of pure acid for tin processing. I always stopped and peered in from the edge. Later, I used to go outside, where I played inside railway trucks and climbed into the steam engine. Dad used to remind me to watch out for the large rats he said abounded there. I never saw any, but they were certainly there.

There were compensations, even for working in such grim conditions. Many people look back on their working time with great affection – and always for the same reason. Catherine Burns says:
I now look back on those days at the Paisely Anchor Mills as the happiest time of my life. I'd go through all the hard work again, for the laughter we shared.

Muriel Weaver, who worked in the London office of a Tyneside heavy electrical engineering firm, writes:
I was fortunate in having wonderful colleagues, even the junior members being conscientious (with a few exceptions), working on after 'knocking-off' time to finish a job in hand even though we had no overtime payment. There was a tremendous 'family spirit' in the office.

Rose Whittle, who worked in the Royal Eye Hospital, adds:
My actual job was Outpatient Records Clerk, but my colleagues and I cheerfully did whatever job was needed at the moment – no argument as to whose job it was – we all got together to work and keep our patients. We had good laughs, more than we can today.

At this time hospital jobs (apart from portering and doctoring, both mainly male preserves) were regarded almost entirely as 'women's work'. Eve Lecomber remembers training as a nurse, which one 1950s woman's magazine described as the 'highest kind of service to which any young woman may aspire':
Nursing in the early 1950s was different from today. Only single girls were accepted for training, and the sister-tutor did not encourage girls to become engaged during their three years as student nurses, but looked for total commitment to a professional career. We were on duty from 7.30am–8.30pm, with three hours off (10–1pm or 2–5pm) and one day off per week. If you were lucky, you might get off duty at 3pm the day before your day off. There was no set time off for study or lectures, which had to be fitted in during off-duty periods. This meant that if there was a lecture in the morning, you would be given 10am–1pm off-duty to allow you to attend the lecture and not disrupt the running of the ward. You weren't expected to miss a lecture: you had to have a pretty good reason for doing so. On night duty we worked from 8pm–8am, twelve nights on and four nights off – and we had to stay up in the mornings if there was a lecture.

It was very hard work on duty. There were no agency nurses, just first, second and third-year nurses plus staff nurse and sister. We spent three months on each ward and got to know the patients very well. On surgical wards, patients for straightforward things like appendicectomy or repair of hernias used to stay for about ten days; others stayed longer according to need. On the medical wards people would be in hospital much longer: a coronary heart-attack patient, for example, would be in for six weeks, beginning with complete bed-rest. Things have certainly changed!

My salary when I started in 1952 was £15 per month gross, £7 net after deductions. Deductions included £6 per month board and lodging, which gave me a room of my own and three meals a day plus morning coffee and afternoon tea. We were not allowed to live out until we were trained. Since most of any social life took place in the hospital and most of us were under twenty-one, we preferred to live in the nurses' home. We had four major dances every year, including the Prize-giving Ball and the Matron's Ball to which all the consultants and their wives were invited. The Catering Officer used to put on a huge buffet with delicious cakes and trifles. We invited young men from Toc.H and City Road Police Station.

On our day off, two or three of us used to go window-shopping in Oxford Street, and would perhaps buy something we'd been saving for – a skirt, for example, for £3-10s-0d (£3.50). In the evening we might go dancing at the Lyceum Ballroom, making sure that we all came home together afterwards. Unless we had a late pass, we had to be in by 10.30pm.

Alan Baker worked for Rothmans of Pall Mall, makers and sellers of 'quality' cigarettes and other tobacco products. Work in the retail trade was just as exhausting then as it is now – and in an 'old family firm' like Rothmans, there were extra demands as well:
When I joined Rothmans, it was still very much an old-established business, with 'Mr Sidney' (Rothman) still at the head. Individual directors had responsibilities for different aspects of the company: Mr Butcher, for example, was the 'Shops Director'. A visit to your 'showroom' (not 'shop') by either Mr Sidney or Mr Butcher was almost like a royal occasion – and I recall that we often received a friendly phone call from someone at head office warning us of an impending visitation. Everything was expected to be 'just so' – and heaven help the branch where it wasn't!

After initial training at the Baker Street branch, I was transferred to Pall Mall. Here, as we were in the centre of Clubland and Theatreland, we served many famous people, who usually bought their cigarettes in 1000s. Rothmans sold their own tobacco products, a range of cigars from all over the world, Ronson, Dunhill and other makes of lighter, and a vast assortment of fancy goods including pipes, cigarette and cigar boxes, and musical chinaware.

As I recall, all branches were open from 9am–5.30pm, with one half-day closing a week, depending on the location of the branch. All branches, apart from the head showroom in Pall Mall and the branch in Victoria Street, were fitted out in the modern manner with glass-topped counters in which to display goods. Pall Mall and Victoria Street were traditional, reflecting the style of shops which must have existed in the 19th century, when the company was founded. They had floor-to-ceiling, oak-framed glass showcases behind heavy oak counters. The light fittings, though electric, had the appearance of large oil-lamps. Until 1953, when cash registers were installed, both branches had cashier 'boxes', again fashioned in oak – and reminiscent of a wooden sedan chair without the handles. Although these were sited by the entrance, and only six feet or so from the counter, the practice was for the salesman to give the customer a chit itemising his or her purchases; this was taken to the cashier, who dealt with the money side of the transaction and returned the chit to the customer to exchange for the wrapped goods. Nothing was ever hurried: if necessary, you could (and often did) spend an hour or more with one customer.

We had a shop porter (a retired serviceman), who was responsible for local deliveries, for taking lighter repairs to Ronson in the Strand, and for packing and posting a wide range of our goods to the customers. Like everyone else, he had his proper place in the staff pecking order. This was well-defined: Manager, First Assistant, Second Assistant, Cashier (the only female), Porter, Cleaner.

In 1956 Rothmans was taken over by the South African Tobacco Company, and launched its products on the general market. All its specialist shops were closed. Alan Baker and his wife decided to leave the firm but stay in the tobacco retail business:
In those days accommodation was not easy to find, so we decided to seek retail management work with living-quarters attached. We started at a combined newsagent, tobacconist and confectioner in West London. The hours were long, and we were expected to run the place with the help of just one part-time assistant in the afternoon. I had to be up at 5.30am to take in the newspapers and mark up the 'rounds' for the paperboys (no girls in those days). I opened the shop at 6am, and we stayed open until 9pm six days a week and until midday on Sundays. We had one day off a week – but it started at 9am, after I'd still had to get up at 5.30am to do the newspapers. After a year, the long hours began to tell and we found another, similar shop in Harringay (now Haringey) where we stayed until 1962.

In the early 1950s Joan Moor, aged fifteen, began working for another old-established firm in London: Swan and Edgar. The layout of the shop, and the attitudes of the staff, were typical of many large department stores at the time:
When I started as a junior I was not allowed to serve customers. I had to tidy stock and dust shelves. After six months I could serve, but only if all other assistants were busy. Each department had a buyer and an

underbuyer as well as the sales staff, and every day the two store managers walked through the store to see that the staff were working properly. There were two store detectives, who walked round the store all day. Sometimes you were asked to serve them so that they could keep an eye on someone they thought might be shop-lifting.

In those days, most of our customers had accounts. The bill was made out, and sent by suction chute to the accounts department. There were also cash tills in each department, and each till had eight drawers. Assistants would have a float, and at the end of the day had to 'cash up' their own drawer. Some of the customers liked the same assistant to serve them each time. You were given quite a few tips in those days – especially from male customers, of which the lingerie department had quite a number. You got to know your customers quite well: one even gave me a twenty-first birthday present.

All stock had to be priced, the tag being handwritten and pinned on. The actual cost and tax were on the back in code. All items for the window displays had to be ironed. Much of our lingerie was pure silk, so we had to be careful. A petticoat-and-French-knicker set cost from £4-19s-11d (just under £5) to about £20. An ordinary nightie cost 15/- (75p), but a handsewn one might cost over £20. An ordinary rayon petticoat cost 10/6d (52½p).

Colin Coupland remembers working in the male side of the clothes business, in an old-established firm in Boston, Lincolnshire:
In those days, only jackets, overcoats and the like were hung on clothes-rails. Everything else was kept in pigeon-hole fixtures, and the smaller items, such as underwear, socks and shirts, were kept in packets. My first job was to dust these packets, check the contents, then refold the packets and put them neatly back in their fixtures. It took a day and a half each week. I will say one learned how to pack a parcel properly: I still use the same method today.

The shop had wooden floors, and there was wooden panelling everywhere. It was very dark. Every morning, we cleaned the floor with sawdust impregnated with linseed oil.

In those days in Boston, 'market day' meant what it said. On Wednesdays and Saturdays, all the shops were packed from 9am–5.30pm, and you couldn't do anything except serve customers. You can imagine what the shop looked like by the end of the day. There had naturally been no time to put anything back when you finished serving, so the stock items finished up piled on top of each other, on all the counters. We spent hours putting everything back in order.

Another big job was window-dressing. We had three windows to do, and used to dress one each week. In those days, the style of window displays was to cram everything in, as tight as you possibly could. Each window used to take two days. The windows were panelled at the back, with a door. Sometimes, if you weren't careful, someone would shut the door on you, and you'd be locked in the window. We once did a Christmas window, packed not only with merchandise but with Christmas decorations, all piled on glass shelves. (Christmas windows always took a week to do, they were so special.) This window was just about finished, when someone tripped on the step going in, and everything collapsed.

The other thing I remember was having our morning tea in the boiler-room, in among the coke. It makes me shudder to think about it now. The stove was antiquated, not large enough to heat all four floors. The top two floors, the stockrooms and workroom, were fine. But the two shop floors were always cold. We used to hate taking things up to the stockrooms, as the building was old and the back staircase was narrow and twisting. Large boxes were particularly awkward – and of course, they got left up there. This meant that every now and then we had to go up and have a clearout. That often used to take a week. I remember once, we thought that instead of bringing the rubbish down all 108 steps, we'd tie string to the bundles and lower them from the window into the back yard. That was fine until the string broke.

Customers in those days were loyal to their shops, so the staff knew and could cater for their customers. Our boss always said that when a customer entered the shop it was because he wanted something, and if you caused him to go elsewhere then that shop was getting your wages.

One of the most frequent comments people make about work in the 1950s is 'Money was tight'. Athough prices were correspondingly lower than today's, so was pay. Harry Lawson recalls that in 1953 he was thirty-four and a local government officer. His salary was £540 per annum. (On the other hand, he points out, he and his wife bought a detached house for £1400.) Mrs A. Saville says that as a shorthand-typist in a building society, she earned £6 per week plus 2/- (10p) a day in luncheon vouchers – and comments 'What riches!' In the same year, 'Su' Bentham earned £3-10s-0d (£3.50) per week as a foreman fitter. Joan Moor gives a perspective on shop-work:
When I began, aged fourteen, I was paid 25/- (£1.25) a week. The

following year I got a job at Swan and Edgar, where my wage was
28/- (£1.40). It was not till I was twenty-one that I was paid the full
adult wage: £3-3s-0d (£3.15). On top of these wages you also got
commission on the goods you sold: 3d (just over 1p) in the pound.

Frederick Walkden says:
Wages were microscopic compared with the vast sums people earn
today. In June 1951 the Ministry of Defence had taken over the
gun range at Eskmeals from Vickers Armstrong of Barrow in
Furness, and I started there in November as a bottom-grade labourer
at £5-3s-0d (£5.15) per week, rising by 2/- (10p) increments to top-
grade (at £5-9s-0d, £5.45) after six months and a show of willingness to
work.

*Harold Mack found living conditions too poor to put up with, and
emigrated to Canada. Here the wages were quite different – and, as he
says, so were attitudes towards 'willingness to work':*
Although in the shipyards where I'd worked in England my job had
been in some ways slow, easy and comfortable – the Union saw to
that – the hours were very long. In a manual job in Canada, if your
starting time is 8am, when the 8am whistle blows, you're there in
overalls ready to push the starting-button of your machine, or dig in
at whatever your job is. The Canadian firms I worked for expected,
and got, their pound of flesh. On the other hand, they paid good
wages: I estimate that in all my jobs in Canada I earned twice the
buying-power that I could have had for similar work in England.

*Howard Palmer remembers how hard-working his Cambridge family
were – and also how enterprising:*
To survive, people often had to do more than one job. My father, a
fitter with the Eastern Gas Board, also did gas-fitting jobs on the side
and worked in the evenings as a waiter at King's College. My mother
worked in a canteen during the day and made gloves at home in the
evenings. My Uncle Len, a chef at King's College, also played the
piano in a band at night. My Aunt Rose worked in the Co-op Dairy
during the day, and sang in a band at night. Even my grandmother
had to work. She was a bedmaker at one of the colleges. She cleaned
the undergraduates' rooms and made their beds.
  As Uncle Len was a chef, one of his perks was the food that was
left over at night, after the undergraduates had been fed. I soon
realised that my aunt and uncle ate better food than we did at home,

so I made up my mind to visit them whenever they had a meal. This paid off handsomely: they gave me plates of the most delicious food I had ever tasted.

The colleges held their May Balls in June. They were called May Balls because, at that time, the undergraduates took their exams in May, and celebrated the end of them in June. Uncle Len's larder was always well stocked because of all the extra food that was needed for, and left after, the King's College ball. My father waited at table at several of these balls each year. (You could work on as many as you pleased as waiting staff were short; he normally did three.) When I woke up in the mornings after these balls there were always stacks of food on the table and in the meat safe.

Even my grandmother got tips from her 'gents' when they left for the summer break. She and her bedmaker friends enjoyed May Ball time because they watched the guests arriving at each college ball, and admired the clothes they were wearing. Dad said she shouldn't do this as it was humiliating and 'belittled the working classes'.

I asked my father why Uncle Len could get all this food as perks and we couldn't. I said, 'Why don't you get perks?' He said that *his* perks were of a different kind from food – and left it at that.

At this point I need to mention that out of the three houses our family lived in (ours, Aunt Rose's and my grandmother's) only one outside toilet was in use, Aunt Rose's. I never asked why there was only one toilet for three houses; it was all I'd ever known. The doors to the toilets for the other two houses were there but were never opened.

About a year after my father told me about Uncle Len's perks, he said that it was time to clear out our toilet and my grandmother's. He brought some sacks home from work, and then opened our toilet door. The whole building was crammed with small pieces of lead, copper and brass pipes. He filled the sacks with all this. It was the same with my grandmother's toilet. I asked him why all this rubbish was in the toilets. He answered, 'This isn't rubbish, it's my perks'. He then took his perks, in many journeys by bike, to sell to a scrap dealer. The metal was saved from jobs he'd been doing over many years.

On another occasion my father did a gas-fitting job, privately, for a dentist in Lensfield Road. The arrangement was that instead of cash payment for the job, our family would have any dental treatment that was needed. This was duly executed by the dentist, and proved to be a painful experience for me. Thereafter I prayed every night that my father never got any more jobs from dentists. Later, my father said he should have charged the dentist more as he'd have liked a gold tooth cap, just like a Pole he knew, who lived in Bateman Street.

10
WHAT TIMES WE HAD!

We travelled miles to meet, queued hours to get in the cinema; shortage of good cigarettes, little choice in sweets, no trips out for evening meals and no TV. We walked and cycled, and after a trip to the cinema we cuddled on the settee. We thought life was heaven.

Dorothy Royston

In a survey at the start of the 1950s, people in Britain were asked what was their commonest form of entertainment. Most men who replied said that their favourite activity was watching sport. Occupations favoured by both sexes included dancing, going to the cinema, and above all – top by a very long way – listening to the radio. Wireless sets (as they were still called) were valued pieces of furniture in most homes, and one of the focal points of family life. Valerie Heath writes:
In the evening we listened to either the Home Service or Light Programme; I seem to remember that we didn't pick and choose too much. Plays, done by the big stars of the BBC Repertory Company, were the best. I liked Mary Wimbush and Richard Hurndall. Another favourite programme was Al Read's comedy show.

Children's Hour was an essential part of life. There were plays like *Norman and Henry Bones the Boy Detectives*, but the best were the drama series: *Bunkle, The Swish of the Curtain*, the *Bannermere* books and historical novels by Geoffrey Trease. The two most memorable to me were *The Box of Delights* by John Masefield and Rosemary Sutcliffe's *Eagle of the Ninth*. This was partly because of their superbly chosen incidental music. For years afterwards, when sitting in a London concert hall, I would suddenly be transported back to 1950s tea time in Yorkshire, as music familiar from a *Children's Hour* play was played. In particular, whenever I hear the savage opening of Stravinsky's 'Symphony in Three Movements', I can still taste fresh Scarborough cod done in my mother's own batter, and remember Greg, with his Canadian sidekick Rocky Mountain, in *Counterspy*.

Valerie Heath's next thought is echoed by all the people who wrote to us about radio. It occupied your mind, but it also left you free to get on with life, in a way TV nowadays does not:
We all did things as we listened, things like polishing shoes, sharpening knives and darning. One of our main jobs was to make rugs, as we couldn't afford carpets. All our clothes and towels were recycled, the cotton-based materials as dusters and cleaners, the more durable material as rugs. We cut them up into small strips, and my parents made a complicated rug with a special tool that could be clipped on and off the strip. I made the simplest kind, using an old clothes peg. One of its 'legs' was cut off and the other sharpened. The sharp end plunged a cloth strip into one of the holes in a cleaned piece of sacking. You held the end that went in and then took out the peg. My mother wanted different shades of rug for different places, but we always needed them too urgently to hoard particular colours, and so they were always mixed.

Like Valerie Heath, Maxine Elvey was a keen listener to Children's Hour – *and to other programmes whose names should stir memories in anyone alive at the time:*
We listened to *Children's Hour* on the radio. There was *Children's Favourites* with Uncle Mac. At the end he used to say, 'Goodbye, children, everywhere'. Favourite choices were 'The Runaway Train', 'How Much is that Doggy in the Window,' 'Tubby the Tuba', 'Sparky's Magic Piano' and 'The Teddy Bears' Picnic'. Other favourite children's programmes were *Toytown*, with Larry the Lamb who made every word sound like 'baa', and *Jennings at School*. *Children's Hour* had a request week every year: you listed your favourite programmes on a postcard and they were repeated.

  Before I started school, and during the holidays, I listened to *Listen With Mother*. This was at 1.45pm, just before *Woman's Hour* (then broadcast in the afternoons). It was always presented by women, like *Woman's Hour*: at the time, most other programmes were presented by men. In *Listen With Mother,* which started with a chimy signature tune, the lady would say, 'Are you sitting comfortably? Then I'll begin'. There would be a story and nursery rhymes. In the afternoon, after *Woman's Hour*, there used to be

Music While You Work. I always associated its signature tune with Mummy doing the ironing. (We said 'Mummy' and 'Daddy' when we were young – till I was about eight or nine – then the less respectful 'Mum' and 'Dad'.) To the signature tune I put the words 'Soapflakes in the soapy water, soapflakes in the soapy water, they are coming, da da da da da da da da da-da-da da-da-da da-da da-da-da-da'.

Sheila Francis remembers a favourite adult programme: Palm Court *on Sunday evenings. In this, a string orchestra played light classical music, with singers (including Anne Ziegler and Webster Booth) and soloists (including Tommy Reilly and Max Jaffa). The members of the Coombes Croft Library Local History Group remember the beloved crooner Donald Peers ('In a shady nook, By a babbling brook'), the top-rated comedy show* Take It From Here, *and especially 'band shows': variety programmes built round star bandleaders and their orchestras. They mention Ted Heath, Vic Lewis, Geraldo and Billy Cotton – and still chortle (they sent us a tape, not a letter) at the thought of the cockney comic Leon Cortes:*
He was very vulgar on the stage, but toned it down a bit for the wireless. He used to do potted versions of Shakespeare, and the Shakespeare Society sent him a commendation because they said he got the basic stories right. Do you remember the Hamlet one – and that line, "E stabbed 'im through the arras'?

Norman Green's letter reminds us that this was still before the era of portable radios (they came in at the beginning of the 1960s). 1950s wireless sets were large, heavy cabinets filled with fragile, electric-bulb-like valves:
I had bought in late 1939 one of the best radio receivers ever made for domestic use in those days. It was a 10-valve GEC 'Overseas 10' receiver and was very luxurious for the time. In 1951 I was afraid (like many other people) that there might soon be a nuclear war, and I thought I'd better buy two complete sets of spare valves for it: there might be long years, as in the Hitler war, when radio was the main means of entertainment and of distributing information. Unlike modern transistors, radio valves wore out, and occasionally had internal faults.

Outside the home, live theatre shows were enormously popular. Almost every large town had a theatre of its own, and cities had several. John Tyrrell remembers visiting the Alhambra in Bradford once a fortnight for a year as a fifteen-year-old, and seeing everything from ballet to Laurel and Hardy, from Gilbert and Sullivan to Morton Fraser's Harmonica Gang. In Dundee, Irene Dowie remembers regular visits from such artists as Frank Sinatra, Mantovani and Alma Cogan. In Liverpool, Sylvia Hulme worked part time in a small hotel frequented by stars who were working at the Empire Theatre, and who preferred to dodge fans by avoiding larger hotels like The Grand. She writes:

I remember Frankie Vaughan drying the dishes for me, Arthur Haynes, Mike and Bernie Winters, and umpteen female singers. The sitting-room walls were peppered with photographs, all black and white and signed. I wonder if they're still there now.

Although major artists did tour the country, the best place to see 'big' shows in those days, just as it is now, was London. There were over forty West End theatres, and as many in the suburbs. Also like today, many West End theatres specialised in big musicals – in those days mainly from America: The Pajama Game, Annie Get Your Gun, Carousel, South Pacific, The King and I. *In 1953 Jane Fabb and her friend Annie had just started work for the first time, in the West End. She tells how theatre-going could be an affordable obsession in those days:*

We went to every First Night for a year. This averaged two or three plays a week – remarkable on wages of £4-10s-0d (£4.50) a week, but we could get into the balcony for 2/- (20p) or 2/6d (25p). We each had understanding bosses who would let us take part of our lunch hour at 10am or 11am when one of us would nip out to the theatre in question and, for 6d, purchase a place on a stool, lined up outside the balcony door. This reserved a place in the queue. After work, we'd take our sandwiches and go and sit on our stools until we were let in, when it was everyone for himself to try and get as near the front of the balcony as possible. It was an education. We saw EVERYTHING, including the first night of *The Mousetrap*! (I don't tell everyone this – it dates me!)

Later in her letter, Jane Fabb explains what teenagers did in the heady days 'BP' (Before Pop):

The *pièce de résistance* was the American Season at the London Palladium for which we had to buy 'proper tickets'. Guy Mitchell, Frankie Laine, Nat King Cole . . . and our favourite Johnnie Ray. We screamed our little hearts out as he sang, wailed and banged his head on his piano. We were speechless for days afterwards (all that screaming) but I don't think I've ever experienced anything as exhilarating as letting rip in company with hundreds of other screaming girls. We autograph-hunted too: I was flung against Johnnie Ray in the crush, and got a piece of fluff from his camelhair coat between my fingers. I clutched it all the way to Charing Cross!

In 1953, another entertainment fashion swept the world – one which now seems as dated as spinning-tops or hula-hoops. By the 1950s, critics were already saying that the 'great days' of the film were over, and movie-makers were resorting to gimmicks of every kind to draw people back into the cinema. Jane Fabb writes:
I see from the special specs carefully preserved in my diary that 3-D films were the latest thing. I remember being terrified watching *House of Wax*.

John Tyrrell remembers the same film:
House of Wax was a horror film (or what passed for horror in those innocent days). Coffins yawned open, skeletons swung out of the screen to grab you, bats swooped past and people menaced you with knives and meat-cleavers. You wore a pair of cardboard spectacles, one lens filled with red plastic, the other with green. This was supposed to give a 3-D effect, so that the nasties were right there with you in the cinema.

Another cinema gimmick of the time was Wide Screen. The Robe, *a Bible epic in Cinemascope, did huge business round the world, and Cinerama documentaries and travel films were enormously popular. But the best-loved films of all were those which offered the simple, unchanging pleasures of attractive stars in interesting stories: hits of the early 1950s included* From Here to Eternity *(which won eight Oscars),* Gentlemen Prefer Blondes *(with Marilyn Monroe),* Genevieve *and* The Cruel Sea *from Britain, and from abroad, Jacques Tati's* Mr Hulot's Holiday *and Ingmar Bergman's* Summer With Monika.

The last two films mentioned were shown in 'art cinemas': small cinemas which then flourished in many large towns and cities. The other films went the round of much bigger buildings. Cinemas in those days were still entertainment palaces, seating as many as 2,000 people. And there were plenty to choose from: in Dundee in 1953, for example, Irene Dowie says that there were twenty-six, all full. Sylvia Hulme says

*that cinema-going was a cheap night out for all the family – and no
wonder, with tickets at 1/6d (7½p), 2/3d (11p) and 3/9d (18p). Jane
Fraser Cross remembers similar prices, and says that many people went
to the cinema twice a week. One member of the Coombes Croft
Library Local History Group remembers:*

Though there were still lots of war films, we were also getting plenty
of musicals in colour (remember *The King and I?*). My friend Jill and
I used to go to the cinema every Monday. Films always used to lift
our spirits. I remember in 1956, at the time of Suez, we were so
depressed – we thought it was going to be another full-time war. But
we went to see *Guys and Dolls* at the Empire, Leicester Square, and
thoroughly enjoyed it. When we came out the crisis was over, and
I've always felt kindly towards that film. We used to go from the
office to the Paramount in Tottenham Court Road. We didn't eat.
We might go in a milk bar for a coffee or a hot chocolate or have
some sweets. Sometimes we'd go to Camden Town (only 1½d bus
ride, 1p), and to the West End if we were flush.

*On Saturday nights, instead of the cinema – or, if you were very
daring, after it – you might go dancing. Jane Fraser Cross says that
the highlight of her week, as for most other teenagers in her area, was
the 'Saturday Night Hop' at the town hall, where for 2/6d (12½p) you
could dance to big-star bands like those of Ted Heath or Nat Temple.
She adds, 'From 8pm–12am the night was mine. But no later: I had to
be in bed by 12.30, or else'. Cedric Parcell remembers these Saturday
night dances – and other occasions too:*

The favoured Saturday rendezvous in Hull was the New York
Rooms – good class and a little on the expensive side at 5/- (25p),
but free of the 'riff-raff' who usually made trouble. At our end of the
city there were friendly little dances every week at the
Goodfellowship Inn. But the best patronised dance hall in Hull
during the winter was the Beverley Road Baths, floored over for
dancing and wrestling (both often the same thing). The dance bands
usually had anything up to a dozen players: part-timers, who
knocked out a lively little rhythm on saxophones, trumpets, piano
and drums. The 'Shilling Hop' in the church hall more often had an
elderly lady on piano and a lad on the drums. Sometimes one of the
top-class professional bands, Joe Loss or Victor Silvester, would
perform a one-night stand, but then the floor was so tightly packed
that the dancers could only shuffle around in the general mêlée.

Cedric Parcell ends by suggesting that, apart from people who enjoyed the dancing itself, there were others who found excellent, if different, reasons for going out to dance:

A lot of fellows who couldn't dance a step went to the Saturday night dance, either for the beer, or because it was *the* place to meet girls.

Many of the people who wrote to us say how entertainment was much simpler, more innocent in the pre-electronic age – and also how much of it was, so to speak, home-made. Sylvia Hulme mentions tea dances, roller skating, coach trips, ping-pong, reading, doing jigsaws and playing family games like Statues or Name the Film Star. Rose Whittle talks of 'many a happy evening with a sing-song round an old piano', and says that 'Saturday night parties were a regular thing, with no violence or trouble and no complaints of noise'. For many young people, church was a main focus of their lives, both for worship and for leisure. Sheila Francis writes of placid, long-gone Sundays:

Most people in the 1950s went to some sort of religious centre each Sunday, sometimes three times a day. Never mind how hot it was, you went along by 2pm and came out at 3.15–3.30pm, taking one old penny for collection. I had to go until I was over fifteen and rebelled (1955), but even then I still went to some evening services.

Sunday evenings meant Church, and after returning, Dad and I would play dominoes, etc., while the BBC's Palm Court Orchestra played on the radio. This was light classical music, and that was all there was. In the summer evenings, people would go and sit upstairs in their front windows, and knit or sew while watching people pass by. I lived on the main road, so we could see traffic too, and in the 1950s I used to play on the road as cars were so infrequent. Summer Sunday evenings saw all the church and chapel-goers pass by in their finery, each one trying to outdo the other with the latest hats – which always had veils and sweeping feathers. At Easter they really went to town on clothes.

Ruth Daly remembers the special occasions organised by churches and chapels in those days, and what fun they were:

My sister and I attended chapel three times a day most Sundays. Our highlights were the anniversary services – infants in the morning, juniors in the afternoon, seniors in the evening. On Whit Monday there was The March. All the local churches and chapels paraded round the villages. Rain or shine. How honoured was the church or chapel leading the march! Each group had its own rousing hymn to sing, so as we all passed each other we tried to outsing our rivals. My sister and I were with the Ebeneezer (English) Baptist group. 'Ebeneezer Lemon-squeezers', the other groups chanted at us. What fun! Of course, the adults took it all very seriously.

In midsummer was our annual outing to Barry Island. Hundreds of Sunday School children, from all denominations, piled on to buses or steam trains (steam trains were the best) with harassed Mams and Dads (mostly Mams).

Another writer, Carol Williams, also remembers those Barry Island outings. In villages, as Marion Olley recalls, church occasions were only part of an incessant bustle of activities, all year long:
There were dances at the Village Hall. The pictures came round on Saturday nights, in a hall near the station, and frequently broke down, when the cheers and shouts started. There were Guides, Scouts and the Youth Club, cricket matches on the field near the station, and a girls' and women's cricket team that was fun, although we weren't the world's best cricketers. We played tennis in a friend's garden, and square-dancing was very popular then. We wore full skirts and the boys wore tartan shirts. We seemed to enjoy life without much money. The church was a place to go, and a crowd of us would go on Sundays, maybe sometimes to see the boys. There were fêtes on the Vicarage lawn, a village show every year to see who had the best marrow and best roses. Sunday evenings a lot of us got on the bus and went to band concerts in the next village. On Christmas Eve we went round with a lorry and a trailer on the back, and a smoking lantern or two, singing carols – or trying to.

On Boxing Day, the huntsmen and hounds all met in the Market Place. The huntsmen, all in scarlet jackets, had drinks from the pub in the market place. Boys went boxing in a pub yard. From this small beginning, I believe, a good boxing club grew, and produced a winner of the Lonsdale Belt.

Even so, pastimes were gradually changing. When Maureen Weitman was an art student in the early 1950s, 'swinging' teenage life was still all duffel coats, hair slides, coffee bars and trad jazz, and Soho was a place which would make anyone who knew the later, seedy Soho blink with astonishment:
This was the great time for Jazz Clubs, featuring such bands as those of Humphrey Lyttleton, Chris Barber and Mike Daniels. Enthusiasts

jived to the early hours, the vigour of life was incessant. Soho Fair
was a prominent feature of the 1950s. Jazz bands played in any
vacant area, glowing with activity and razzmatazz. Soho became a
fairyland; coloured lights decorated the streets. The 'Two I's' coffee
bar arranged tables and chairs on the pavements, and soon other
cafés joined in. Festive mood was apparent; jive and the zest for life
were in full swing.

*Nothing could remain as uncomplicated as that forever. Or as innocent.
In 1955, Sylvia Hulme says,*
I recall the song 'Lay Down Your Arms' being banned (as it might
encourage desertion among national servicemen), and another record,
'The Creep', which had been played in dance halls, being banned
because it was 'too suggestive'. We kids didn't even know what
'suggestive' meant.

*Radio Luxembourg, Bill Haley and the coming of Pop soon put a stop
to that! Sheila Francis says that, like millions of others, she was soon
'bopping' to 'Elvis the Pelvis' (whom she describes as 'rather
suggestive'), and to his English equivalents Cliff Richard (whom she
calls 'young, handsome and wholesome') and Tommy Steele. The
teenage explosion, in whose fallout we still live, had begun: transistor
radios, 45rpm records, extravagant lifestyles (Teds, Mods, Rockers) –
things would never be the same again.*

*In cinemas and dance halls another change was taking place. In the
mid-1950s Bingo swept the country. It was cheap, cheerful and
appealed to millions. Cinemas and dance halls were converted for
Bingo, and the popularity of those two former staple entertainments
waned virtually overnight. In 1955 ITV began, which led to ratings
battles and a huge expansion (and some would say deterioration) in
home entertainment.*

*Of course, some things did not change. For half the male population
of the country, and hundreds of thousands of its mothers, sisters and
girlfriends, Saturday was still the day for football. Brian Garner
writes:*
In the early 1950s I was doing national service, but I still managed to
see most of Spurs' games in the midlands and north. Army pay
wasn't fabulous – 28/- (£1.40) per week for the first six months – and
I hitched or travelled on a platform ticket to the matches. Before the
match I always made for a 'National Restaurant', where you could
get a three-course meal and tea for 1/10d (9p). Soldiers, pensioners

and childen were admitted to most grounds for 9d (3½p). Programmes cost 1d or 2d each.

*Harry Lawson still remembers the Blackpool–Bolton match on 2 May
1953 as if it were yesterday:*
The final score was Blackpool 4, Bolton 3. Bolton, leading 2–1 at
half-time, lost Bell injured. But he came back on and scored their
third goal. In my opinion, Mortensen 'turned' the match. Blackpool
were losing 3–2, when he scored with a direct free kick. This left the
way open for Blackpool to storm forward and Matthews' pass found
Perry who scored the winner in the last few minutes. The Queen
presented the cup.

*Another major change was on the way: holidays. For most ordinary
people during the war and during the dreary years of rationing which
followed, holidays were largely out of the question. If you were lucky,
you went for a day trip with your church, youth group or works. This
was especially fun for the children – and everything about the
experience was amazing to them. Carol Williams recalls the sheer
excitement of it all:*
Once a year our Chapel used to go to the seaside. The whole street
used to walk up to the railway station a few miles away to board the
train. The excitement we all felt as children was tremendous, and
when the steam train roared into the station, everyone (mums and
dads included) let out a loud cheer. When the train approached the
sea, we all shouted, 'There's the sea, there's the sea', as if we'd never
seen water in our lives before – but after all, it was only once a year
we went down to the seashore! When we got there, the feel of the
sand, the smell of the salt in the air and the waves rushing over us
was sheer bliss!

*Sylvia Hulme remembers similar excitements, on holidays arranged for
the young people at her children's home:*
The train journey was an enormous thrill: sitting on the upholstered
seats, white lace on the headrests, and with framed pictures of
country scenes screwed to the compartment walls.
  The holiday place was usually a seaside resort. Clean beaches,
donkey rides, Punch and Judy shows, beach games, buckets and
spades, beach balls, icecream, deck chairs. These simple things
seemed to suffice everyone, two weeks every year.

We used sometimes to go to the Isle of Man, crossing on the ferry *King Orrey* (where all the children but me were seasick). On the island, volunteer families took as many children as they could accommodate: usually two each, or three if there was another brother or sister. They made us welcome, and the council laid on trips.

But travel, too, was changing. Until the mid-1950s, most people in Britain kept themselves to themselves, avoiding Europe and hardly ever going further afield. But restrictions gradually eased, and foreign holidays became cheaper and more available. Some people struck out on their own. Joan Harper and her husband had a motorbike and sidecar, and had previously gone on touring holidays to the Lake District and Cornwall. Then,

. . . towards the end of the 1950s we discovered that my husband (who was a railwayman) could get cheap travel on the Continent, and decided to try Tyrolean holidays. We went there in 1958 and 1959, and found so much unspoiled beauty.

Peter Simmonds worked for Thomas Cook, and gives fascinating details of where people used to go, how they travelled there, and what it cost, in the days just before the first jet aircraft and the first package tours:

Travel to the Continent was booming. But charter flights were few and far between, and holidaymakers were still travelling by train to most destinations. Special holiday trains, run by a consortium of travel companies, operated on a weekly basis to Austria, Switzerland, Italy and Spain. The trains had a limited number of couchettes, but seats were predominant. I remember that a restaurant car was attached to the Swiss train in Basle to serve breakfast (which had to be prebooked before departure). On the return journey, breakfast was taken in a large hall in the docks of the French port. Uniformed staff from the travel firms rode in each train to give general assistance to passengers.

Holidays to these countries cost from £25–£45 for a week. Destinations further afield cost more: Gibraltar, Malta and Cyprus cost from £72–£138. Nine-day or ten-day coach tours to France, Belgium, Holland and Switzerland ranged from £34–£42 per person.

Two ships were launched in May 1953: the Orient Line *Orsova* of 28,200 tons and the P&O *Arcadia* of 28,000 tons, both for the Australian trade. Although at the time these shipping companies were competitors, they were later merged into the P&O Line we know today. Also in 1953 motorists could fly their cars across the Channel by Silver City Airways.

We complain of fare increases on the railways today, but in May 1953 French Railways increased all their fares by a massive 25 per cent.

11

GETTING ABOUT

A smart new train, 'The Elizabethan', was to inaugurate a
breathtaking, new, fast service to Scotland, and the entire
school was dutifully marched in a crodocile across Mill
Common to see it thunder through Huntingdon Station.

David Dixon

*If we could travel back in time to 1950s Britain, the most astonishing
thing would probably be the almost total lack of cars. On a typical
town estate of 100 families, only two or three might own cars – far
fewer in poor areas and in the country. Cedric Parcell remembers that
in 1950s Hull bikes, not cars, were the rule, and that 'everybody, even
the manager of the Labour Exchange, pedalled to work'. He continues:*

Blue-and-white trolley buses ran smoothly along our roads, as yet
not clogged to a standstill with thousands of cars, and the horse-
drawn cart was still a fairly common sight.

*Ronald Coley also remembers the frequency of buses, and comments in
passing that 'the queues were orderly and well mannered'. Sylvia
Hulme, writing of 1950s Liverpool, lived in a children's home some 12
miles from her mother's house. She recalls:*

The fare (on the tram) was 6d (2½p), and if I walked I could keep
the money. This I did one day a week, Saturday. On that day, we
were 'free' from the home from 10am–7pm. By the time I'd walked
to mother's, I was often exhausted, but happy to see her, and my
younger brother.

She continues:

There were few cars on the road in those days. Indeed, few roads
were wide enough to take cars.

Writing of Colchester forty years ago, Molly Schuessele takes up this point:
By the early 1950s, the town was starting to expand. Where there had been farms within two miles of the town centre in all directions, new housing estates were going up. The increase in houses meant very soon an increase in traffic down the roads into town, which had been built originally for horse-drawn vehicles. So the council was brewing many plans to ease the traffic flow.

The shop where I worked was in the middle of a row of about fifteen shops at the end of Maldon Road, a main artery into town. By 1951 the traffic problem was becoming a nuisance. The road was so narrow that if only one van or lorry was parked outside the shop the traffic was jammed up for a long way. This was of no use to the shops: nobody could stop to do business there. So in 1952 my employer was told that his property would be pulled down and a new road system would be made. (In fact the road system wasn't finished until 1974, twenty-two years later.)

Peter Poole remembers his journey to school in Devon, by train, ferry and 'Shanks' pony':
The under-sixteen rail fare from Brixham to Paignton was 3d in old money (1½p), adults 6d (2½p) – and in those days Brixham was still connected to the main-line railway system by means of a branch line from the main line at Churston. This line was operated by a little ex-GWR tank locomotive, and there was just one coach. It was known to locals as the Whippet. Once you reached Churston, a journey of about six miles or so took you to Kingswear, the terminus, and you then boarded the railway ferry (the Mew, of just 117 tons, built in 1908), and crossed the River Dart. You then had a long walk up to the school (the long-since vanished Dartmouth grammar school). At the end of each day, this journey was repeated in reverse.

Mr Poole adds:
I often smile nowadays when my own son, aged nearly sixteen, complains about having to walk any distance!

David Dixon remembers cycling, for pleasure, along miles of empty lanes in Huntingdonshire – not to mention along the old A1:
Although road traffic was gradually increasing as more and more new cars became available, it was still possible to cycle along the Great North Road for miles on end and see barely half a dozen cars

in the course of an hour. On the lanes and bridlepaths we were lucky to see the odd tractor, though as I remember even the minor roads were kept in excellent condition. Equipped with Esso road-maps we pedalled the length and breadth of the county, with snacks and drinks neatly placed in saddlebags, along with toolkits and the essential puncture outfit. Road safety was of little concern, for although I did recall being given a somewhat gruesome little colouring book containing pictures of boy road casualties, I only had one relatively serious accident when a stray dog jumped in front of our wheels as we were freewheeling down one of the few hills in the county, and in the collision that followed my friend David Wollard split open his chin on the road and had to have stitches.

Older riders, like Cedric Parcell, could make even longer journeys – though they, too, were not without their risks:
The summer we moved house I bought a motorcycle and sidecar. Beryl's brothers were motorbike enthusiasts at the time, and it was partly with their encouragement that I was persuaded to buy a 500cc Norton. Attached to the bike was a black, coffin-shaped box which Beryl immediately christened the 'hearse'. With many protests she squeezed herself into it and sat Pamela on her knee. When I dropped the lid on them we were out of communication. No matter how loudly she shouted I couldn't hear her. One day on a trip to Bridlington Beryl set the contraption on fire. The cigarette-end she thought she'd thrown out of the window, had somehow blown back into the torn upholstery of the seat and smoke began to fill the hearse. Beryl frantically banged on the lid to attract my attention, and I had to stop by a ditch and scramble down the bank with Pamela's toy bucket. Thereafter the hearse became a no-smoking vehicle.

Rena Brewin's family also had a (remarkably sturdy) motorcycle combination:
We all used to travel on it: Dad controlling the whole thing, big sister on the pillion, Mum on the front seat of the sidecar and me on the back seat. Where did we put the luggage when we went to stay with relatives? In the sidecar with Mum and me!

People's memories of public transport in London vary. The ladies of the Coombes Croft Library Local History Group recall:
You used to get buses and tubes running late in those days. If you

went to a show in the West End, you'd come out at 11pm, and you could always get home.

On the other hand, Joan Moor remembers inconvenience:
We're hearing all the time now how crowded the London Underground trains are, and people are saying that London Transport must get its act together and do something. What has changed? I might tell you that the Underground was just as crowded forty years ago.

12

DEATH OF GEORGE VI

I am not usually one to show emotion in public, but I was by no means the only person there with tears running down their cheeks.

Peggy Close Riedtmann

King George VI died on 6 February 1952 – and many ordinary people felt personally bereft. Peter Ryde (a secondary schoolboy at the time) puts such emotions into perspective:

I remember hearing the news from another boy, at school, just at the start of a French lesson. I was very sad about it. Not that I was particularly struck on the Royal Family, but George VI was always rather special to me. I thought he had a lot of guts to take on a job for which he was ill prepared and totally unsuited, and to end up doing it so much better than likely. (Which is no more than to say, I suppose, that he was the patron saint of younger brothers and ugly ducklings who still hoped they might turn out to be swans.) But in a way which I still find it quite difficult to explain, he seemed to embody the sort of courage and true nobility which really count. He had a fundamental decency and natural, unaffected dignity which you respected and admired not because someone said you should, but because you wanted to. He had seemed a good sort of person to have around, and I reckoned I would miss him. We were invited, but not instructed, to wear black ties to school for a fortnight, and quite a lot of boys did so.

Other young people took the news more coolly. John Tyrrell remembers being given the day off school – and spending it improvising hours of 'solemn music in C minor' on the piano, until his (normally placid) mother threatened to leave the house and never come back. Evelyn D. Riegert and her friends took the news as the chance for a treat (which never in fact materialised):

We went to school that day, but were given the day off because 'the King was dead'. Many of us went to the ice-rink to skate – but when we got there, it too was closed because 'the King was dead'.

To Bryan Taylor and his young colleagues in the RAMC band at the time, the King's death brought a welcome change in routine:
I remember that no music was allowed to be played for two weeks, but at least it meant that we didn't have to go on parade.

Another young man, Harry Molyneux-Seel-Unsworth, was serving aboard a destroyer in the Korean War. He recalls:
We were told that the King had died, and were requested to donate 2/6d (12½p) each out of our pay towards a memorial which would be erected in his memory. If it ever was built, we were never informed.

At David Dixon's secondary school, back in Britain, the pupils were so surprised by the news that at first they were reluctant to believe it was true at all:
News was broken by the headmaster, Mr Stevenson, who interrupted the morning's lessons to pass on a bulletin from the BBC. At first we half expected it had to be one of Stevenson's jokes: after all, he had disturbed lessons the previous year by wandering through the school asking everyone to name the shortest night of the year, and informing his bemused staff and pupils alike that the answer was Sir Gordon Richards. This time, however, he really was in a sombre mood. We discussed probable reasons for the King's demise. Most of us put it down to the fact that he had only one lung, and so could only logically have expected to live half a normal lifetime.

Younger children were even more bewildered. Howard Palmer recalls the King's death as just one of the events (perhaps the key event) in a confusing day:
I was at St Matthew's Infants School, in Norfolk Street, Cambridge. We were in class and had been given paper and wax crayons to draw with. Miss Cripps, the teacher, had told us that we could draw anything we liked, which was unusual as we normally had to draw something of 'educational value', such as a vase of flowers.

I was sitting at the table next to a boy called Williams. He said, 'Let's draw the war and fight battles and kill Jerries'. I'd heard of the war, of course, but this was the first time I'd been invited to take part in killing Jerries, so I readily agreed. Williams was bigger than me, so he decided that I could draw all the dead Jerries while he drew the goodies (whom I supposed to be the English). I drew a dead Jerry on my bit of paper, handed it to him and he drew the goody who had shot him. Then I drew a Jerry on his bit of paper, and he drew the triumphant goody. After a while, this drawing game began to seem stupid. I was about to suggest to Williams that we each drew whatever we liked on our own pieces of paper, when another teacher threw open the classroom door and almost ran to where our Miss Cripps was seated. The teacher, I forget her name, was crying and holding a hanky to her nose. She whispered something to Miss Cripps, who reeled back on her chair and said, 'Oh no! When did this happen?' More whispering from the other teacher, then 'Shall I tell the children?' from Miss Cripps. By now there were 60 little eyes on the pair of them. The other teacher, who was elderly, looked up at us, tears welling from her eyes, and said, 'No, let the poor dears hear it from their parents. Let them all go home now. Miss Franklin said it's all right'.

When we heard this, and even though we didn't understand why Miss Franklin, the head teacher, had said we could go early, jubilation entered our little hearts. Miss Cripps said, 'Put your papers in the bin. You may all go home. Something terrible has happened'. The warlike Williams immediately put his hand up and asked 'Have the Germans invaded us again?' Miss Cripps assured him that they'd never invaded us during the war and that their current status ensured it would not happen in the foreseeable future, God willing. With that we were all sent home. Those whose parents normally collected them were allowed to play in the sandpit until their parents arrived.

I didn't live far from the school, and I always went and returned home on my own. When I got home my mother told me that the King had died. Now, I knew we had a King, but I couldn't remember him or what he looked like and I told her so. She said, 'He's on every penny. You must remember him'. I said I didn't. She went to her purse and looked through the money in it, trying to find a coin with the late King's likeness on it. This attempt to enlighten me was not a success, as she only had coins with the head of George V, the late King's father. She then said that I'd probably seen a picture of him in the newspaper but had forgotten about it. This presented me with a problem which needs explaining.

Every Saturday, my father collected all the old newspapers and cut them into small squares with my mother's pinking shears. (She made leather gloves at home, as an outworker for a local glove factory.) He then sorted them into manageable bundles, pierced a hole in each

The heart of the Coronation ceremony. In a ritual dating back more than 1000 years, and watched by selected representatives of Church and State, the Archbishop of Canterbury raises the crown to place it on the young Queen's head.

Rain-hats, mackintoshes, umbrellas, military capes – essential wear for a British Coronation in 1953.

Princess Anne, accompanied by an attendant, watches the procession from a window of the Palace. Anyone who was, or knew, a child in the 1950s will recognise her hairstyle immediately.

The lions in Trafalgar Square were ideal places from which to watch the processions – but only for pigeons. In a scene straight from some Ealing comedy film, crowds turn their attention from the main event while a policeman talks down a human reveller.

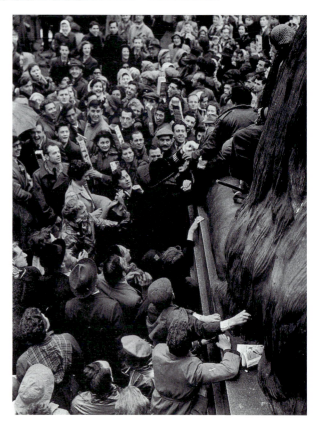

Everywhere they sang
the National Anthem

THOUSANDS PEER.—And thousands cheer from their periscope view points in Trafalgar-square.

Daily Mail Reporter

THE splendours of this Second of June at
ston Chu~~rchill said b~~
Queen

Several London papers, including the *Daily Mail* (whose photo this is) gave away
cardboard periscopes: wonderful, until the rain began. *Daily Mail* caption: 'Thousands
peer, and thousands cheer'.

Advertisers cashed in on the Great Day. Coach-built prams like these lasted for
generations – for babies, and as buggies and go-carts for older children.

The newly-crowned Queen, and the Duke of Edinburgh, riding in the State Coach at Hyde Park Corner.

Bird's (or Nelson's) eye view as the procession passes through Trafalgar Square. The sea of spectators filled the square: at least fifty times the number of people shown here.

Cecil Beaton's formal photograph of the newly-crowned young Queen. This photo was once seen in every embassy and consulate throughout the Commonwealth.

One for the family (or Family) album: the Queen, with Prince Philip, the Queen Mother, Princess Margaret, a serious Prince Charles and a spectacularly bored Princess Anne.

The Royal Family on the balcony of Buckingham Palace.

Britannia, as played by Frederick Walkden's daughter in her school pageant. The costume was a miracle of improvisation – as Mr Walkden reveals on page 170.

Official programme for the celebrations at Sherburn near Scarborough. Like most towns and villages, Sherburn had been planning its Coronation Day for nearly 18 months, since the King's death in February 1952.

SHERBURN

Elizabeth R
1953

Coronation Celebrations

June 2nd

Souvenir

CHURCH SERVICES.

Sunday, 31st May, 1953.

Special Coronation Service, 6-30 p.m., at the Parish Church.

Tuesday, 2nd June, 1953.

Wesleyan Chapel, 9 a.m., Short Service.
Parish Church, 10 a.m., Short Service.

FANCY DRESS PARADE.

Judges : Miss Johnson, Belgrave House, Scarborough and Mrs. B. Duckworth, Staxton.

Stewards : Messrs. Duggleby, Newton, Wilson, Pratt and W. Ward.

Judging will take place outside the School.

SHERBURN BRASS BAND will accompany the Parade.

Route : Meet at 2-30 p.m. Church View then Parade to The Cross, St. Hilda Street, High Street, Springfield Terrace to the School.

Sherburn Parish oners only to compete.

Classes :
Prettiest - (1) Children   (2) Adults
Comical - (3) Children   (4) Adults
Most Original - (5) Children   (6) Adults
Decorated Vehicles - any vehicle - one class (7)

Each child entry not winning a prize - 6d.

First Prize 10/-; Second Prize 5/-; Third Prize 2/6 :- All Classes

Entries : (Before the day please) to Mr. Wadlow, Sherburn.

TEA PARTY.

At 4 p.m. (Approx.)

CHILDREN. At Sherburn School.

All children up to 15 years of age or in last term of ordinary School (Filey), except babies

Parents must bring young children and collect them again after tea. The members of the Committee will look after the children during the tea.

Bring mug and spoon.

OLD FOLKS TEA In the Wesleyan Chapel Room.

Lady Pensioners over 60 years with their husbands.

Gentlemen Pensioners over 65 years with their wives

Names to Mr. Marston at the Post Office please.

Where necessary, transport to and from the Tea will be provided, but in these cases, would requests for transport be made before the day.

PRESENTATION
BY
Mr. AND Mrs. NEWTON
OF
SOUVENIR MUGS AND SWEETS TO ALL CHILDREN
OUTSIDE THE SCHOOL
AT 5-30 P.M.

All Children at the Party and Babies

SPORTS.

In the FOOTBALL FIELD at 6-30 p.m.

Open to Sherburn Parishioners only.

Entries : To Mr. Newton, Sherburn School (as soon as possible please.)

OFFICIALS

Judges :   Judges Stewards :
Mr. M. T. Barstow.   Mr. A. L. Duggleby.
Mr. C. S. Curry.   Mr. Wilson.
Mr. W. Ward.   Mr. A. Stead.

Starter : Mr. F. Stones   Starter Stewards : Mr. Newton.
Sport Secretary : Mrs. M. Charter   Mr. R. Metcalfe.
Recorder : Miss J. Grice.   Mr. Pratt.

First Aid : Equipment available at Secretary's tent.

Music : By Sherburn Brass Band.

CHILDREN.

EVENT No. 1. Children under 5 years. 25 yards Flat.
1st 2/-.   2nd 1/-.   All others 6d.

EVENT No. 2. Children 5 years but under 8 years.
Boys. 60 yards Flat.   Girls. 50 yards Flat.
Sack Race   40 yards Skipping.
1st 3/-.   2nd 2/-.   3rd 1/-.

EVENT No. 3. Children 8 years but under 11 years.
Boys. 80 yards Flat.   Girls. 80 yards Flat.
40 yards Sack.   40 yards Skipping.
Mixed High Jump.
1st 3/-.   2nd 2/-.   3rd 1/-.

EVENT No. 4. Children 11 - 12 years.
Boys. 100 yards Flat.   Girls. 100 yards Flat.
40 yards Sack.   40 yards Skipping.
Mixed High Jump.
1st 3/-.   2nd 2/-.   3rd 1/-.

Programme cover for the celebrations in Colchester. This was a classy production: ninepence in 1953 (4p) would have bought a cinema ticket, a large loaf, or a packet of fish and chips.

The Coronation Queen and her attendants at the village fete of Bingham, in Nottinghamshire. The Queen is Anne, the attendants are Marion and Hazel, and the 'coach' is a decorated railway lorry.

Maxine Bonner (then aged 7) as a soldier at a Fancy Dress party in East Ham, London. The splendid Herald on her right carries a pennant with the Coronation Crown.

bundle with a meat-skewer, threaded string through the holes and tied it in a loop. The bundles were then hung on a nail in my aunt's outside toilet, which we used. The problem I had was that the only time I came into contact with newspapers was when I used the toilet – and to add insult to injury, I always looked for a face on a piece of newspaper to finish my ablutions with. Faces meant little to me in a newspaper; I couldn't read anyway.

At length my mother sent me to my Aunt Rose's house to watch *Children's Hour* on television. Unfortunately, on this day the BBC had cancelled all programmes as a mark of respect to the dead King. This upset me terribly as it was the night for Muffin the Mule, which I enjoyed.

Later that evening a cow escaped from the Co-op slaughterhouse in York Street, made its way to our back garden and demolished our garden shed. Dad was pleased with this occurrence, as he said he would claim money off the insurance for a new shed. We had chicken for Sunday dinner that week.

Some days after the King died, all the children at St Matthew's Infant School walked to the allotments behind York Street, where we could see the train carrying the dead King from Sandringham to London. The train was bedecked in black material and Union Jacks, with soldiers wearing fur busbies standing every few yards along its length. The patriotic Williams, with whom I'd had the drawing game, said, 'Let's pretend they're Jerries'. We did this, shooting them all with imaginary Sten guns. A boy called Nicholas began to cry because he'd never been so close to a steam train before and the noise frightened him. The rest of us laughed at him. No one liked him because he was the only one in the class who could read.

The Coombes Croft Library Local History Group remember the same procession passing through London:
It was a dull day, just like the Coronation later. Every window was decorated beautifully, with flowers and mourning. Some windows in the West End had pictures of the King, usually mauve-draped. I remember the Duke of Kent in the long, solemn procession. He was very young and gangling, and looked a bit of a fool. But he tried ever so hard, so you started off laughing and then you felt sorry for him.

The King lay in state in Westminster Hall. Elisabeth Brooke remembers her father saying that queues of visitors were four miles

long. Peggy Close Riedtmann was one of those who queued; she
describes the scene once you got inside:

The catafalque was covered by the Standard, with the Orb, Sceptre
and Imperial Crown on top of the coffin. Gentlemen-at-Arms and
Yeomen of the Guard stood with bent heads, hands on sword-hilts,
so still as to seem like statues. There were flowers strewn all along
the carpet down the centre of the hall where people had dropped
them as they moved slowly by and out at the far end. The only
sounds to be heard were those of feet treading so quietly – it was
terribly moving, and I understood for the first time Dickens' almost
obsession with footsteps, ghostly and otherwise, in his characters'
lives. Everything about the scene was awesome: the shimmering,
glittering royal jewels on the coffin, the resplendent uniforms, the
ordinary folk of all ages and places and the unearthly quiet. A great
many people wore a touch of black: usually an armband, scarf or
hat.

13

EVEREST

On 29 May, 1953 Sir Edmund Hillary and Tenzing Norgay became the first to reach the summit of Mount Everest. Many people remember hearing news of the achievement:

My only memory of Everest is that this was the time that I became aware that things could obviously be stage-managed to fit occasions, and that the news had been deliberately held back to coincide with the Coronation. From then on, I think, I distrusted PR people.

Robin Ollington

All during the Coronation procession, the BBC kept reminding us that Everest had been conquered. We felt so happy, and so proud to be British. It put the seal on a wonderful, wonderful day.

Arnold Bamfrith

I remember hearing about the conquest of Everest on Coronation Day. Afterwards, speaking to my father about this, he said, 'The British are the best in the world, we are the only ones who could have done it'. And I agreed. But when we went back to school after the Coronation, I was horrified to find out that Edmund Hillary was a New Zealander and Sherpa Tenzing was Nepalese. I told my father. He said that the Sherpa didn't count as he was only doing his job, and Hillary was as good as English as he came from New Zealand, and anyway his name was of English origin so that made him English. At the age of seven, this made sense to me.

Howard Palmer

My friend's daughter had the best reaction. She was only six, and was staying with a friend while her mother went to watch the

Coronation. When the mother got back she went in and said, 'Sue, here's a cup of tea. It's raining, and they've climbed Everest.' Sue was all dopey, and she said, 'Oh. Perhaps they'll see it better from there.'

Grace Peary

GOD SAVE THE QUEEN

Elizabeth Alexandra Mary, eldest child of King George VI, succeeded her father on 6 February 1952. She was the great-great-granddaughter of Queen Victoria and the namesake of Queen Elizabeth I – two of most highly-regarded monarchs in British history. She was young (twenty-five), a happy wife and mother, and popular. The monarchy itself, after being rocked by the scandal surrounding Edward VIII, had recovered its reputation in the time of her father, who had been revered for his unassuming dignity and steadfastness during the Second World War. Although in 1953 there were a few Britons who muttered about the unearned wealth and privilege of the House of Windsor, and talked republicanism, the majority of the population seemed to be unquestioningly royalist. Indeed, one newspaper survey at the time revealed that two thirds of those questioned believed absolutely that the Queen was directly related to God.

So far as national self-image was concerned, the Coronation could not have come at a better time. The country was just beginning to climb out of its post-war misery: a brave new future was about to dawn – and to be christened, by popular newspapers, a 'second Elizabethan age'. David Dixon writes:

As the Coronation came into prospect, the mood of the whole nation changed. Previously only the Festival of Britain had inspired such talk of a bright new world for the nation, but as the month of June approached it was clear that this was to prove far more significant than either the Skylon or the Dome of Discovery.

So the idea was born, and government plans were laid. The Coronation was to be, as usual, a solemn state and religious occasion. But it was also to be a massive national party, a shout of goodbye to the past and welcome to the future. Mrs F.E. Hamill catches the mood exactly:

It was to be the 'the greatest show on earth', a celebration of Empire

107

where 'the sun never sets', bringing together for perhaps one last time people from nations all across the world who wished to see the Queen crowned, and all united in the simple pleasure of taking part . . . It was a little bit of glamour and extravagance too – and everyone welcomed and enjoyed that.

14

GETTING READY

One detail which sticks in my mind is a lamp on the top of the National Gallery, flashing the message 'Long May She Reign' in Morse code.

Donald Burling

If no one but grandees had taken part in the Coronation, the whole thing would have been simple. Those invited – foreign royalty, diplomats and members of the British establishment – amounted to less than 10,000 people. Even with their guards, outriders and other attendants, they would have been far fewer than, say, the average Saturday crowd at Wembley Stadium. But there were also millions of others to consider: spectators from Britain, visitors from every part of the world, and the innumerable radio listeners and film and TV watchers.

If grandees only had been involved, the walk (or ride) to the Abbey need have taken only some twenty minutes: along the Mall, through Admiralty Arch and down Whitehall. But because of the spectators, it was extended to some ten times this length: out along the Mall, Northumberland Avenue and Victoria Embankment to the Abbey, and back via Whitehall, Pall Mall, Piccadilly, East Carriage Drive in Hyde Park, Oxford Street, Regent Street, Haymarket, and back down the Mall to the Palace: total marching time (estimated) one and three-quarter hours. At every point along the route, preparations had to be made for the watching throng. Statues and fountains were boarded up; the streets and buildings were hung with flags, crowns and other decorations which were a spectacle in themselves; stands and barriers were erected.

As Coronation Day approached, such preparations grew more and more frenzied – and the number of sightseers seemed to double and redouble with every passing hour. London soaked up visitors as a sponge sops up water. Everyone was good-tempered and willing to put up with discomfort and chaos. But how long would it be before the city was completely full? Barbara Allman remembers the crowds in the streets, and in one hospital as far out as Lewisham:

I was Head Physiotherapist at St John's Hospital, and lived in residence there. Naturally everyone wanted time off around the time of the Coronation, to witness the preparations and arrival of the hundreds of royalty and dignitaries, the procession itself and the festivities which followed. The situation became almost cut-throat, culminating in the drawing of names from a hat.

London itself and miles around were completely chaotic. Three days before the Coronation, it was impossible to get through Lewisham and to the City. Traffic was jammed everywhere, and at 4pm on Coronation Eve the roads were closed and sealed off. Nothing, but nothing, could move. Hospital staff who lived out could not get to work, and those at work had to stay. Doctors and other staff were crammed into every inch of space on the premises, trying to catnap while sharing chairs.

Margaret Mackie was one of hundreds of thousands of people for whom a day out to see the preparations was almost as great a treat as Coronation Day itself:

My friend and I went to see the decorations. My sister had been the day before, and had impressed upon us that if we saw nothing else we must go into Westminster Abbey. Now, in those days I was a person who could walk miles, but was inclined to go faint if called upon to stand. None the less, we queued to get in for about one and a half hours, and it was worth every moment. I shall never forget the beauty and dignity of everything, especially the gold and blue chairs for the important people.

Peggy Close Riedtmann went into town on Sunday 30 May. She wrote this account at the time, to give a detailed picture to relatives who lived too far away to make the trip themselves:

We went by bus to Hyde Park Corner, and walked along Constitution Hill to the Palace. Apsley House was completely hidden by stands. There were hundreds of people milling around. We could hardly get anywhere near the Palace, but took a couple of snaps from the Victoria Memorial, looking up the Mall. We went under Admiralty Arch, which was wonderfully decorated with anchors, and knotted ropes in intricate designs, and via Trafalgar Square, down

Whitehall. There were more decorations here, and Horse Guards Parade in particular was fine. I was struck to see gorgeous fresh flowers blooming everywhere, both in beds and in crown-shaped baskets on the walls of buildings. We had a look at Parliament Square – or what was left of it with all those huge stands. It made me think of the days when they had pavilions built round the jousting arenas, and I quite expected knights in armour to appear. We walked down Victoria Street, all gay in red and yellow, and caught a bus home.

In the evening we did a further trip, and saw Eros in his gilded cage. We were almost caught in the ghastly crowd waiting to see the visiting royalty and others who were being entertained at a theatre there. First the police pushed the crowds back, and then the crowd reversed the procedure and, cheering wildly, sent the force the other way. I've never seen anything quite like it, and was glad we weren't in it. We beat a hasty retreat, and after walking all along Piccadilly and Park Lane, crept exhausted into the Dorchester for a much-needed restorer.

Visiting London on the same day, Joyce Brandreth also found the crowds amazing. (Her account, too, was written at the time.):
On Sunday last we were up early, and Tony took us up to Town to have a good look at the decorations. It was a lovely morning. Hundreds of others were up early also, and Hyde Park Corner was jammed more than on a weekday at 8.30am. Westminster was packed. They were putting out the flowers in Parliament Square – it looked grand. We crawled in a queue up Whitehall; the Mall was too packed, so we didn't attempt that. In Oxford Street we got out and walked. It was then about 8.15am, and just as crowded as a normal lunch hour. The decorations were really super, I wish you could see them, but I expect you'll see some on the films.

Part of the confusion in the streets themselves was caused by long lines of cars, filled with sightseers – more vehicles than had ever been in the capital at any one time. There were even bus tours to see the decorations – and Mary Underhay's great-uncle, Captain Jackson OBE, took one of them:
We thought that Fleet Street was the best decorated, with streamers of all colours, and crowns which seemed to be floating in the air. Selfridges had a full-sized figure of HM the Queen on horseback, and

Liberty's windows, decorated with period costumes of the various kings and queens since 1400, were marvellous.

If you worked in one of the prestige shops along the processional route, you were exceptionally busy in the weeks and days before the Coronation. All shops decorated their windows and frontages – and many rearranged the insides entirely, to offer viewing facilities on the day to favoured customers. Alan Baker was 'Second Sales' at Rothman's head showroom in Pall Mall. He writes:

Because the showroom was right on the processional route, the Rothman directors decided that it would be an excellent vantage point for themselves and selected guests on Coronation Day, and plans were drawn up to gut the property and erect a stand of raked seating in the shell of the original shop. Fortunately the firm owned a small shop property in adjacent Royal Opera Arcade. This was quickly redecorated and, a few weeks before the big day, we moved lock, stock and barrel from our imposing Pall Mall showroom to our new temporary home.

Although the 'new' shop was cramped and inconvenient, the move was all part of a very exciting few weeks. As the showroom was dismantled and the seating and decorative drapes appeared so, all along the route, the flagpoles, flowers and special set pieces were being erected. I spent several lunch times walking through from Pall Mall to the Mall to watch progress being made on the giant fairy tale arches with the huge coronets suspended from them. As the date approached, it was almost as if a 'coronation fever' had taken hold. At home in Shepherds Bush, bunting and flags were going up throughout the streets of terraced houses, and arrangements for street parties were well under way.

As Alan Baker says, it wasn't just 'posh' London which was putting on a show. Similar preparations were going on, and similar decorations were going up, in other parts of the capital, and all over the country. Maria Wrist writes:

In Fulham, where I lived, there was a festival atmosphere. Shops competed with each other over the decoration of their windows and fronts, and I can still visualise Putney High Street with all that red, white and blue. Ordinary houses, too, were decorated. Pictures of the Queen and Prince Philip looked out of front-room windows, and again the colours of red, white and blue dominated the scene.

In Glasgow, as Pat Miller recalls, there was even a 'best-dressed' competition:
Decorations in red, white and blue were everywhere. The shop windows were terrific. I recall Copland and Lye's windows in Sauchiehall Street most vividly. I believe, from memory, that Raglan Street at St George's Cross won a prize for the best-decorated street in Glasgow, or maybe in the whole of Scotland.

Colin Coupland was working in a men's outfitters in Boston, Lincolnshire. He remembers one of the many 'struggles and problems' he and his colleagues had in decking the front of the shop with flags:
It was a tall, four-storey building. We had a very large Union flag but no flagpole, so we got a pole and pushed it out of the workroom (second-floor) window. Then we tied it to the bench at which the tailors and alteration staff worked. Most of the staff sat conventionally on chairs in front of this bench. But we did have one Italian tailor, who sat cross-legged on the bench, just where we put up the flagpole. He therefore had to sit on the pole – which was fine until the wind blew, and he found that the pole was slowly sliding out of the window.

In schools, residential streets and homes, people were also busy. Howard Palmer was a small boy at the time, unsure of the meaning of what was going on, but enjoying the out-of-the-ordinariness of it all, and accepting (in a child's unquestioning way) whatever came along:
Months before the Coronation, the teachers at our school had us drawing Union Jacks, orbs, sceptres, maces and golden coaches, to instil into us the importance of the event. Even now, the sight of red, white and blue brings back images of the Coronation. Lots of kids had cardboard periscopes, which were advertised in the papers 'as necessary for complete viewing of the Coronation'. (In fact only one boy from our school actually went to the Coronation, and he told us afterwards that it rained so much that his cardboard periscope collapsed, and his mum later used the mirrors that were in it when she put on her make-up.

Local areas often held competitions for decorating streets and houses – and sparked all kinds of ingenious ideas. Gillian Bark (also a child at the time) remembers the standard flags and bunting, together with pictures of the young Queen, and then goes on:

Someone made a picture of the Coronation crown on their front lawn out of beer-bottle tops. I much admired this.

Diane A. Noble was nine and a half, and at primary school. She writes:
I made up a cardboard cut-out model of the Coronation coach and horses, and this was put on the small table in the front-room window, along with an arrangement of red, white and blue streamers.

Val Hastings, then a teenager, was her family's artist-in-chief – with excellent results:
Our street decided to hold a whole day of events, including a house-decorating competition. Weeks before, my mother acquired some white muslin, and I remember we decided to decorate our house (a semi with bay windows) purple, gold and blue. (We wanted to be different from red, white and blue, and Mum said purple was more regal.) She dyed the muslin in her washing machine, and we draped it under the front window bay and the downstairs bay windows. Then I painted a lion and unicorn in the middle pane of glass downstairs, with a coat of arms, and a rose, daffodil, thistle and shamrock in each corner. We put photos of the Queen and Duke of Edinburgh on the two upstairs windows, and flags and rosettes over the front door. Dad planted the borders around the front lawn with red, white and blue plants. We won first prize: a small cup which I still have in my cabinet.

Putting up decorations was, perhaps, the most noticeable kind of preparation for the great event. But behind the scenes, a thousand other things were going on. Some of them – like this reminiscence from Margaret Robinson – were entirely sensible when you think about it, but at first they sound more like Alice in Wonderland than real life:
I lodged in Palmers Green with a fashion student whose jobs were to sew spots on the ermine on Coronation robes and pockets into the robes specifically for sandwiches. The side of the robe the pocket went depended on which side of the Abbey the wearer was allocated.

While an army of dressmakers, cooks, printers, vehicle-repairers, grooms and equerries bustled about their business, people from the real army were also hard at work. Men and women from the forces were to march in the procession, line the route, fire ceremonial cannon and play in dozens of marching bands. All this needed careful planning, and hours of practice. Mrs V.E. Glazebrook was a member of the WRNS

(Wrens), and was one of those chosen to march in the naval contingent on the day. She recalls:

Selection took place in April: two Wrens were chosen from each shore base, about 60 in all. We were not told until later what we had been selected for.

At the beginning of May we reported to HM Barracks at Portsmouth, to start intensive training. We were introduced to our instructor CPO who had to knock us into shape. He spent the next few weeks shouting, bullying and cajoling until he was pleased and proud of us. The schedule was aimed at making us fit for the thirteen-mile march on 3 June:

Monday	1.10–2.15	Squad drill
	2.30–3.30	Physical training
Tuesday	8.30–9.30	Physical training
	1.15–3.30	Marching six abreast
Wednesday	8.30–10.20	Route march four miles
	10.45–11.20	Physical training
	1.15–3.45	Marching twelve abreast
Thursday	8.20–10.40	Route march five miles
	1.15–3.55	Squad drill twelve abreast

– and so on, increasing every day. We spent the evenings nursing sore feet and stiff limbs. We treated our feet with surgical spirit to harden the skin, polished our shoes, and brushed and pressed our uniforms until we met the high standard needed.

On the last few days Portsmouth and Southsea were treated to a preview. The whole of the Coronation Navy Contingent took part: Royal Marines, Royal Navy, Wrens, bands. People came out of houses and shops, left the beaches and lined the route. I remember writing at the time, 'I felt as if my body was too small to contain the proudness I felt. It has made the hard work worth while'.

William Davies BEM, a serving member of the Royal Navy Reserve, was one of six men chosen to represent the Reserve lining the Coronation route. Like Mrs Glazebrook, he spent days beforehand in physical training, hardening the muscles for the eight-hour stand in Whitehall on the day. He adds a memory which shows just how pompous and mindless officialdom could sometimes be forty years ago:

We were amused by a notice which went up on the barracks board. It read that all ratings taking part in the street-lining should refrain from drinking alcohol and from sexual intercourse for at least forty-eight hours prior to the day. At the time we were several hundred sailors in a barracks, with no shore leave and no contact with women. Not only that, but the canteen bar stayed open until 10.30pm. Who dreamed that up?

Bryan Taylor, a member of the Royal Army Medical Corps (RAMC) Band at the time, remembers a gruelling schedule of practices and physical training – though not without its funny side:

In January 1953 we learned that the band was to take part in the Coronation procession, and long-distance marching practice started straight away. At first it consisted of marching round the camp several times a week, leading the RAMC contingent of troops. But as the weeks went by, the distance was extended and we marched for miles round the country lanes, much to the surprise of the people in the villages of Crookham, Crendall and Ewshot.

Normally, as we marched, we played each march twice through then went about the same time without playing. This was because on the big day, we would be massed with three other bands, but only two bands would play at a time. The other bands were Princess Patricia's Own Royal Regiment of Quebec (of whom, we were to discover on the day, only one man spoke English!), and two RAF bands. We were eight across and sixteen down, forming a band of about 120 musicians.

I remember that sometimes when we were marching without playing, the cows in the fields, being inquisitive creatures, would run to look at us; but, much to our amusement, when the band struck up it scared the living daylights out of them, and they ran away in panic. I often wonder if there were any farmers puzzling over the loss of milk-production from their herds.

The next stage of the exercise took place about two weeks before the Coronation, when we went to the Guards Depot at Pirbright in Surrey to join up with the other three bands and practice marching under the watchful eyes of Guards drill-sergeants. I remember that the Regimental Square was lined with guardsmen practising standing still for hours on end. They would be lining the Mall, shoulder to shoulder, on the day.

A few days before the Coronation, the band moved to Earl's Court, where we were to stay. Earl's Court was packed with thousands of servicemen, who seemed to be permanently blancoing and polishing. We had two-tier bunks to sleep in, and even as we were trying to settle down, lorries kept driving in and out of the huge building, delivering more beds and tables.

The morning before the big day, there was a front-rank rehearsal. This entailed the front rank of each band – in our case it was basses and euphoniums – marching round the whole route so that we'd know which side of traffic islands and monuments to go, and how to split up to go through Hyde Park and Marble Arch. To avoid too much disruption of the traffic, that rehearsal started at 4am.

15
TAKE YOUR PLACES, PLEASE

It seemed as if all London had turned out to watch, as well. As I was only seven years old and not very tall, I could see nothing but other people's backs. I started to wail, rather loudly, so I am told, much to the annoyance of my older sister. A kindly policeman took pity on me, and after asking my mother's permission, hoisted me on to his shoulders for the duration. Of course I immediately stopped fussing.

Genie Carson

For most people working in central London on Coronation Day, an early start was vital – in some cases, as early as the day before. Peter Simmonds writes:

I was employed by Thomas Cook and Son Ltd, and for the Coronation that company had built a stand at Apsley House in Piccadilly. Members of staff had been asked to volunteer for duty on the day, as stewards on the stand and as escorts to passengers arriving by train with reservations to view the procession. Hotel accommodation in London was completely booked, and many overseas visitors had been accommodated in ships at Southampton and other ports. On the day itself, special trains were run to bring people to London, arriving very early at termini. These clients were then escorted on foot to the stand, by staff carrying placards identifying each group.

I was one of those selected to be a steward on the stand. As we had to be on duty from 6.30am, arrangements had been made for us to sleep in the firm's head office in Berkeley Street, and mattresses and bedding were provided in the typing pools. Our early-morning call was the constant ringing of the telephone by the switchboard operators, who had been on duty all night, and after a good cooked breakfast in the staff canteen, we made our way to the stand, a matter of five minutes' walk away.

My job was to inspect tickets on one of the entrances. Clients soon started to arrive. Loudspeakers in Hyde Park and along the procession route constantly relayed the BBC announcements, interspersing them with playings of the National Anthem. As the majority of the seat-holders for our stand were overseas visitors, they could not understand why we stopped work during the playing of the anthem – all the more so because it was raining and they were becoming uncomfortably wet.

The Pullman Car Company was providing meals for everyone, and long tables were laid out in tents for the customers' breakfast snacks. Packed meals were provided for their luncheon. Underneath the stands, rooms had been built amongst the scaffolding for the use of the clients, and TV sets had been installed for them to view the Abbey ceremony. The staff was also catered for: a buffet service was provided in our own room, but no TV. We could however stand on the seats and look over the dividing wall into one of the clients' rooms and see the screens, though not very comfortably. In fact, once all the clients were seated to watch the procession, many of the staff went under the seating and, by cutting the hessian fronting to the stand, we could sit on the scaffolding and have an excellent view over the heads of the standing crowd. Indeed, some of the clients came and joined us, saying that they could see better from under the stand than from the seats they had booked.

Gwen Heath worked for Middlesex County Council at the Middlesex Guildhall in Parliament Square, just across the road from the entrance to Westminster Abbey. Like Peter Simmonds, she was employed on the day to look after dignitaries – and remembers out-of-the-ordinary sleeping conditions on the night before:
Our marvellous location had been put to good use: scaffolding stands had been erected on the front and side of the building. The Clerk of Council's Personal Assistant, for whom I worked, was responsible for the allocation of the seats to the county councillors, justices of the peace and other important people, and so we were embroiled in the exciting run-up to the great day. On Coronation Eve we slept in the offices; while not particularly comfortable, we were at least better off than those camping outside on the pavement. In the morning we used the rather limited washing facilities in the basement. An overzealous head porter started showing in the early arrivals while we were still only half-dressed.

Our main duties were showing people to their seats and handing out programmes. Then, when exciting things started to happen, we found the best vantage point we could for ourselves.

Marion Bunting was a secretary working for the Rank Organisation. She writes:
Rank had been running Coronation competitions all over the country, and the winners were invited to spend the day at cinemas throughout the region, including at the Haymarket Cinema, Piccadilly.

The winners came from far and wide. They had to be at the cinema very early that day, and the prize consisted of a slap-up breakfast, a superb luncheon and afternoon teas. Of course, the drink was free and flowing.

The start of the Coronation activities was shown in the cinema itself on a large television screen. The actual procession was due to take place later in the afternoon, and seats had been laid out on the cinema steps so that the winner could sit outside and get a magnificent view of the procession.

Two colleagues and I were asked along to the cinema to help with the refreshments, and to see that everyone was well taken care of. However, as there was a team of waitresses laid on, we were really surplus to requirements. We had the breakfast, watched the television screen, enjoyed the lunch. The winners were mostly northerners – and I'm afraid that by the afternoon they'd had so much to drink that they weren't capable of going outside to watch the procession: most were asleep in the cinema! Since so many seats were not taken up by the winners (who were past caring whether they saw it or not), my two companions and I were able to have a first-class view of the entire procession, sitting in the winners' seats.

Pamela Bowen and her parents were among the guests lucky enough to be entertained by one of the large London companies. Their day started with an early-morning train-journey from Kent to London. Pamela Bowen goes on:
We had to be at the P&O Passenger Office in Cockspur Street by 7am. Seats were arranged in tiers in the main windows of the offices, and there were marvellous views of all the various activities which went on prior to the main procession. While we were served breakfast by stewards from one of the P&O passenger-ships, we watched horse-drawn coaches and carriages going by, either empty on their way to collect people or containing people of note *en route*

to their allotted position in the parade. How lucky we were to be in the dry, for we looked out onto rain-soaked streets. I remember particularly watching the guardsmen's bearskins getting wetter and wetter as the day wore on, and wondering how they would be able to stand so still with what must have been very heavy weights on their heads.

Joan Moor worked for Swan and Edgar in Piccadilly – and Coronation Day found her being treated just like one of the company's honoured guests:
Swan and Edgar was a department store, which had lots of windows opening on to Piccadilly and Regent Street. Some were sold to private individuals. But others were kept for the management, or were allocated to members of staff who had worked for over five years. This last group included me.

I was given a ticket (which I still have). It stated that I had reserved accommodation at Swan and Edgar, and was to reach my destination by 8am. On arriving at Piccadilly Circus station, I had to produce my ticket, and the police would give me facilities as far as prevailing conditions would allow. When I arrived, just after 7am, there were crowds everywhere. Many people had been there all night. I managed to get to an office window facing Piccadilly Circus, and took two photographs of all the crowds. It was 7.30 in the morning. I was then shown by one of the managers where my window was. It was at the side of the buildings in Regent Street. There were other members of the staff there too. The Underground station was closed at 9am. I thought I might be in for a long and boring wait, but there was so much going on. People were dancing and singing, and everyone was in a joyous mood.

For P. Bryant, getting to her reserved seat in time involved complicated manoeuvres the night before:
My sister Nancy was a Westminster Hospital sister who was to be on duty at the Abbey. She had to be there at an extremely early hour to be advised of her duties. We decided that she would smuggle me into the Nurses' Home and we'd share her bed. Goodness knows what would have happened if we'd been discovered! When she left for the Abbey I had to disappear before the maids came in to do the room. So I ensconced myself in a loo with a paperback. The minutes passed very slowly, until at last I could leave and make my way to my seat, right opposite the main door of the Abbey.

For many of the people in the streets, camping out was one of the main pleasures of the occasion. Rachel Jones and her mother, in fact, camped 'in', on iron bedsteads (relics of fire-watching during the war) in huge public dormitories in the Ministry of Defence. Geoffrey W. Shardlow camped on the kerbside grass near Green Park, 'near the toilets and opposite the Duke of York Monument'. He remembers two nights and days of 'drinking tea, singing, enjoying the revelry and the atmosphere'. Ernie Rumsey was a young secondary-school boy. He and his cousin made their move early – and thought that they'd done very well for themselves:

We left home at about 9.30pm and after a lot of walking we found a very good position on a corner, so that we could see well to our left and to our right – and we were in front.

On the presumption that we must know something they didn't, a crowd soon formed behind us. The consequence of this was that with the barrier in front and the people behind, we only had room enough to sit down on a wet pavement in a crouched position.

Never mind, we were going to witness a grand spectacle, in close-up. When dawn broke I did become quizzical about some white markings in front of us, but as time passed with nothing happening, I relaxed.

It was about half an hour before the procession was due, when they arrived: SIXTHFORMERS, ten feet tall and five feet wide, and lots of them, taking up position in front of us, so that we could see neither ahead nor left or right. They really must have been hand-picked for size.

The procession arrived. My cousin and I stretched so that we were standing on our toes in the ballet position. Providing the person in the procession was on horseback, we could see his helmet. We did see the Queen's coach-driver (what a thrill!) because he was higher up – and we saw the top of the coach itself.

So there we were, tired, miserable and with cramp in our legs. We gave up, staggered home, slumped on the armchair and went fast asleep – and didn't see anything on television, not even in black and white. The best laid plans . . .

Muriel Weaver and an ATS friend from Yorkshire camped on the pavement itself: 'the only occasion,' Muriel Weaver writes, 'apart from queuing overnight for Wimbledon, when I "slept rough" on the London streets'. She goes on:

On the afternoon of Coronation Eve, after stoking up with a hearty meal at home, we set off with sleeping bags, food and Thermos flasks of hot drinks. There were already crowds milling around, and we claimed a spot just off Trafalgar Square, near Admiralty Arch, from which we thought we'd get a good view. It really was a wonderful experience as the crowd, getting denser and denser, was in such a jolly, good-natured mood, so the time passed quite quickly. There were jovial policemen, buskers to keep us amused and numerous vendors of food, drinks, etc., continually passing, and many a humorist in the crowd raising plenty of laughter. Needless to say we didn't get much sleep that night, though we did doze off from time to time.

We had to get up on our feet quite early next morning when the crowd got thicker and kept pushing from behind, surging and swaying back and forth. But no one complained, taking it all as part of the wonderful occasion. When news came through on the loudspeakers that Hillary and Tenzing had reached the summit of Everest, one forgot all the weary feet, stiff legs and cricks in the back, to cheer and cheer and cheer.

When the Guards arrived to line the route, we didn't think we'd get much of a view. But in fact, when the procession did arrive, we were lucky to be able to see across into the Square and into the carriages. I was even able to get a quick snap of the Queen, though rather distant.

Pamela Barnett was an undergraduate at Lady Margaret Hall, Oxford, and she and a group of friends spent the night in the Mall. Sleep was the very last thing on their minds:
There was plenty to interest us: the beautiful decorations, especially the archways with suspended crowns in the Mall, and our fellow-members of the crowd. I particularly remember some Americans who celebrated a joyous reunion with their daughter, there on the pavement: cries of 'Honey child!' It poured with rain, but that didn't seem to matter. In the early hours of the morning we did some Scottish dancing in the middle of the Mall: *Petronella* and an Eightsome Reel.

Mrs J. Ashenden (then ten years old) and her school friends put their waiting-time in the Mall to a different – and mischievous – use:
We chatted to the policemen on duty, gave them sweets, and disposed of the sweet papers in the belts and bayonet cases (at least I think that's what they were) of the poor guardsman on duty. I often wonder how much trouble he got into when he got back to barracks.

Another young person who spent the night in the Mall, Geoffrey Gardner, also enjoyed crowd-watching. People were so tightly packed, he says, that at one point he dozed off on his feet, too crammed against other bodies to do more than slump. Mrs B.M. Woulds remembers another problem in the Mall, which the huge numbers didn't help:

I needed to spend a penny, and I'll never forget being in a crush, trying to get back to my sister, with a dirty old man pushing himself at me. He disappeared as soon as a policeman came into view, but it was still awful. When I got back to the Mall, it was to discover that the police had made everyone get up and move back. I was panic-stricken, thinking I'd lost my sister, but fortunately we found each other again.

Jeannie Barnes also remembers 'needing to spend a penny' and the crowds, for a very particular reason:

My first child was due to be born on Coronation Day. Some magazines were giving away baby clothes and prams to any baby born 'on the day', so I felt very disappointed when my son was born ten days late. However, it did give me a chance to mingle with the crowds and savour the wonderful, colourful atmosphere in London, although my husband was concerned in case I went into labour. My only worry was the length of the queues to the public toilets. They seemed to stretch for miles! However, people were very kind. They took one look at me, large as life, then passed me on to the head of the queue.

People in the parks had more space – but only just. Phoebe Ames remembers:

A friend with four children had asked me if I'd like to see the Coronation with her and her four children, sleeping out in Hyde Park overnight. I'd said I would. Her sixteen-year-old son and I had 'held our stand' with macs, rugs, cushions, etc. from four o'clock on the afternoon before. Meanwhile, Marjorie had ferried food to us from a house in Regent's Park, and just before the gates at Marble Arch were closed, had arrived with the other three children: one boy and two girls, the youngest about nine.

We had a merry night. I was the 'bolster' against which the children propped themselves, and we dozed fitfully, entertained by students from a Drama School camping next to us, who rehearsed songs and parts of plays plus quite a lot of horseplay. In the early hours we heard the newsboys shouting that Everest had been conquered, and soon afterwards police and troops began lining the route. We divided into two parties for the purpose of visits to toilets. One party held the fort while the others went off.

Soon the police warned us to keep our places. The smaller children kept to the front, behind gaps in the route-liners so that if a surge of people behind came, they would not be knocked over. We couldn't sit any more, in case we were trampled as the crowd built up behind us.

We were in reserved seats near Marble Arch. Soon after we were seated a young couple arrived with their six-year-old daughter. They had only ONE seat. They had chosen to have their child occupy the position for the day. They promised to come back for her and told her not to be afraid, even though she wouldn't be able to see them in the standing throngs further down the street. She was a lovely child, well groomed, good mannered and with great poise. She and our daughter, aged seven, soon became 'chums for the day'. The two little girls sat between my husband and me, sharing a lap robe. Little bare knees would be warmer there. We listened to the ceremony on loudspeakers in the trees – and when the procession began, we were almost near enough to touch the coaches as they passed. At the end of the day, we remained with the child as the stands emptied around us, until her parents returned for her. I wonder if she ever remembers the Canadian family who watched the Coronation with her on that memorable day.

Mrs D.J. McDonald

Molly Hames travelled all the way from the Midlands, and spent a slightly more comfortable night (though she got little sleep):
I was a schoolteacher, and for years I'd collected National Savings from my classes. As a reward I'd been allocated two Coronation seats in Hyde Park, opposite Apsley House. I didn't own a car, and my headmaster offered to take me in his.

We set off about 10.30pm on Coronation Eve. I'd packed several meals for two – supper, breakfast, lunch, dinner – with flasks of hot and cold drinks and sherry, port, etc. to drink toasts to the Queen. I wore a grey flannel suit with a blouse and jumper, so that I could disrobe or dress up according to the heat of the day. In those days I still wore a hat and gloves, thank goodness, and I also took a mac and hood, and a beautiful car rug which was supposed to be waterproof. We had maps, and permits telling us where to park in Sussex Gardens.

I remember that the whole area was manned by police brought in from all over the country, so that if we enquired the way, we were told 'I don't know, I've never been to London before'. But we found our parking place, and after eating our supper we settled down in the car to try to sleep. It was very cold – no car heaters then.

About 4am we woke to the sound of happy voices and smell of sizzling bacon, and found that most of the people parked by us were up and breakfasting. We ate bacon sandwiches, and got out to stretch our legs. Everyone was in a very gay mood. It looked like being a beautiful day. We had to be in our seats early, so we left the car and walked across. We were soon settled comfortably, with an excellent view and ready for anything. We had blow-up cushions, macs, umbrellas, rugs, cameras and plenty of food. I don't remember when it started to rain, but despite all our waterproof clothing and umbrellas we were soon soaked to the skin. We kept our seats to the bitter end, but it was so wet that we didn't bother much about food. I enjoyed watching the soldiers eating by numbers. Each had his little packet of sandwiches, and it seemed as if the officers were saying, 'Up, bite, down, chew'.

Biting and chewing, though not necessarily to numbers, were activities crucial to Doris Matthews and her employers. Not everyone had brought their own food; not everyone was as lucky as the soldiers Molly Hames watched. For everyone else waiting on that cold, damp day, Doris Matthews' firm of multiple caterers provided an essential and very welcome service:

Specially designed, gaily decorated pavilions were set up, complete with outdoor seating and kiosks for the sale of cigarettes and icecream. Once the decorations on the route were completed, thousands of visitors came to see them, and the catering programme operated, I believe, for about ten days before Coronation Day itself.

By the evening of 1 June, all was prepared for a great summer celebration. The pavilions and kiosks were well stocked, as all the approach roads were closed to vehicles. All the staff working at these points spent the night there, making themselves as comfortable as possible. Anyone who lived through Coronation Day will knew that it was very cold and wet. By 6am we had run out of hot food and drinks, and as access was closed it was impossible to re-stock. One intrepid manager tried to get through with a case of tea or coffee, but was stopped by the police.

The pavilions were positioned well behind the area reserved for the general public. So, although we were close to the route, we saw nothing of the procession. I did glimpse the top of a feathered head-dress as one carriage was heard to pass by!

Harry Ashford was one of the NAAFI officials in charge of 'special catering events', providing 'biting and chewing' materials for the troops. He remembers:
I ordered 27lbs of mustard (3 × 9lb tins) for the cheese mix we used, going by the NAAFI recipe for a said number. But because of the taste, we used only 6lb, on 36,000 rolls, half the total used. As each man got two rolls, there were 72,000 in all. They were baked with special flour to stay fresh, and came from NAAFI bakeries in Aldershot, Ludgershall and Portsmouth, among others. The second roll for each man was meat. I recall we used brown paper bags for 'normal' meals and white paper bags for some overseas troops who needed different food – or maybe it was the other way round. Barley sugar and other items were packed into the bags. These bags were for the mid-day meal only. It took about 48 hours to prepare the food, and the bags had to be ready and sent out from our Mill Hill site by 5am on the day.

In the Garrick Hotel in Leicester Square, Arthur Brand worked just as hard, and saw even less. But in days when a waiter might earn as little as £2 per week, there were compensations:
I was a lounge waiter: my job was to serve drinks in the lounge bar. For three days I worked double shifts, staring at 6–7am and finishing sixteen hours later. Two of us worked each shift. Most of our customers were foreign visitors to the hotel, or important people staying for the Coronation. Although some tips were small, sixpences and threepenny pieces, over the three days as a whole I made £87 in tips, a fortune. When it was all over, I slept for two solid days.

Work of a considerably different – and much less financially rewarding – kind was done by Rosemary Miller. She was a young policewoman from North Yorkshire, sent to London some days before the Coronation for special crowd duties:
We stayed at the Women's Section House in London. At 6am on Coronation Day, we were transported to New Scotland Yard, and were briefed about which positions we were to have. The Embankment had been reserved for schoolchildren, and I took up position in front of them there, together with some Royal Marines. It

was cold and wet the whole day. Blanco from the Marines' helmets ran down their navy-blue jackets. But everyone who was going to the Abbey passed our way – and how the children cheered and clapped!

Ellen Poole and Eileen Fry were two of those children. Ellen Poole remembers:
I was fifteen, and went to St Marylebone Central Secondary School. A few weeks before the great day, we were informed that two people from each class, one male and one female, could go to see the Coronation. We would view it on the Embankment, along which the procession would pass on its way to the Abbey. Names were put into our form teacher's hat. To my amazement mine was picked out. The other was 'Trog' (as he was nicknamed), one of the nicest boys in our class. I liked him a lot. We were told to be at school at 6.00am on the big day.

On the day I packed sandwiches and a mac, kissed my Mum, little brother and big sister goodbye and walked from King's Cross, where I lived, to school near Marylebone High Street. It was quiet. There was no traffic. We took the Underground to the Embankment and were placed near one of the tall trees on the opposite side of the road from the river bank. We had plenty of room to move about.

Eileen Fry writes:
All the schoolchildren from our area had to be assembled on the station at West Croydon by 6.45am, to catch the special train. My Dad escorted me on my bike to the station: very few people had cars in those days. As the train left, he waved me off, and I waved back, clutching my sandwiches, and a bottle of drink packed in my brown leather school satchel.

The train arrived in London and we were marched along in lines to our designated spot along the Embankment. We were there by 7.30am. We had a long time to wait, but the moments passed quickly, and there was always something to see and talk about. By coincidence the boy who lived opposite me in Ringwood Avenue was also close by. We'd been playmates in our early years, and when we were five had walked along to school hand in hand. This was now an embarrassing memory, and we hadn't actually spoken to each other for about five years. But today was different, and soon we were chatting together. We knew that at home our families would be sitting around the television set. But we were on the spot, and were determined to make the most of it.

The weather was cold for June, and it drizzled now and again, but this did not dampen anyone's spirits. I've never seen so many happy smiling faces. Preparations were taking place all the morning. Policemen and cars whizzed about, and street sellers were everywhere selling flags and periscopes.

What Eileen Fry remembered as 'drizzle' bulks a little larger in other people's memories. Gwendolen Piggott remembers holding out the cup of her Thermos to catch drips from the umbrellas round about. There were no umbrellas round Pat Freestone, and the rain teemed down: 'Umbrellas would have been very bad manners where we were, as they would have stopped other people seeing. But most people used newspapers for a little protection.' Audrey Berry's sandwiches were so sodden with rain that she couldn't eat them. Margaret Jarrett and her friend had 'wavers' (sticks with red, white and blue streamers), and before long found the dye coursing down their arms as the rain soaked through. Sheila Wilson remembers that the crowd's favourite songs, played by the bands again and again while everyone joined in, were 'Singin' in the Rain' and 'It Ain't Gonna Rain no More, no More'. As for bandsmen, Bryan Taylor writes with feeling how, halfway through the procession, they had to stop for five minutes in Hyde Park to upend their instruments and pour out 'a considerable amount' of water. And Bob Hallowell, one of the Canadian servicemen brought in to line the processional route, has a very glum memory of English weather in 'flaming June':

I remember well standing in Cockspur Street in London, freezing wet, watching my ceremonial sword turn rusty. I was part of a Canadian contingent designated to take part in lining the streets of London, as opposed to marching, and I'd have preferred the marching – it would have been warmer! The reason my sword turned rusty was lack of training on the weapon. The ceremonial swords had only been issued two days earlier; mine was a Mark VI George. We'd carefully cleaned them, but no one had told us that the final touch was a thin layer of Vaseline to prevent rust.

Jane Fabb (then a teenager) and her friend Annie were lucky enough to be under cover, in Parliament Square. To judge by this account – which Jane Fabb wrote at the time – they seem to have used the occasion for some serious soldier-spotting:

We had a wonderful position, in the front row directly opposite the annexe door through which the Royal Family were to enter the

Abbey. We didn't realise just how good it was until they arrived because we thought they'd go in through the front door. We got to the stand about 5.25am, and just sat watching the people. I'd taken books to read but didn't look at a single one all day. It was a very cold, wet day. We were wearing our winter coats and fur boots, and were luckily under cover. Behind us were some colonels who were in charge of telephones through which they spoke to other officials along the route. A wing commander was next to Annie, also with telephones, trying to decide whether or not the planned flypast could take place, due to the terrible weather. A lovely Guard with blue eyes sat to our right, announcing items to the people in the stands. He wore a uniform with a silver metal helmet with gold trimming and a white horsetail tassel. There were crowds standing on the pavement below us, rows of police in front of them. Then there were the Guards and some RAF men who stood for the Guard of Honour.

About 6am, peers and peeresses started to arrive, in their red velvet and ermine robes, carrying coronets. One peer dropped his coronet which bounced musically along the pavement. When he bent to pick it up, his packet of sandwiches fell out. Cleaning ladies kept appearing and sweeping the carpet leading into the Abbey. They got a cheer from the crowd each time.

Two further letters, from Patricia and Peter Elcoate and from Peggy Close Riedtmann, take us through the early part of the day, from setting out from home to the beginning of the procession – and capture the good humour, bustle and excitement of the time. Mr and Mrs Elcoate were newly engaged, and were due to emigrate to Canada at the end of the summer. They were determined to see the Coronation, a last glimpse of British pomp and ceremony, before they left – and so:

. . . despite dire parental warnings about the crowds and how it would be impossible to see anything, we awoke with the dawn chorus and met before 6am in a parking lot a few minutes from Reading Station. Arriving in London by 7am, we took the Underground from Paddington to Marble Arch, with our map of the parade route in our hands and a vague idea of where we wanted to be. The trains were not overcrowded at that time, but there were already many people established on the pavement, while others, like us, were finding their spot.

We selected a raised bank beside Park Lane. Despite the hundreds already there, we had what turned out to be a good position, as we settled down for a long wait. More and more people were arriving to join the good-natured throng. There was little to entertain us except the goings-on in the crowd itself. The road had been closed to traffic since dawn, but we raised a cheer for what was a rare sight in those days, a jogger, and a thunderous applause for some dustmen on a truck, who acknowledged with exaggerated bows and waves.

Having broken fast at 5am, we ate our sandwiches well before lunch time, but were sustained by refreshment booths set up in Hyde Park, where toilet facilities were also available. The weather remained overcast, the clouds regularly letting down a thin drizzle which prompted many of the bystanders to fashion hats from the morning newspapers, or from anything else which came to hand.

Neither of us can remember how long we waited before the procession came by. Time passed and we were together. Eventually a naval contingent arrived, and took up positions at intervals on the roadside. The crowd had swelled considerably, but we could still glimpse the road ahead of us. The papers had made us very familiar with who was in the procession: leaders from many countries and from our own government and armed forces.

Peggy Close Riedtmann went with her sister Daphne and friend Doris. This account was written at the time:
I had to go to the office on Monday, but Doris met me for lunch, and then I dashed home in the evening. Daphne was busy packing up mountains of provisions, and Doris and I both bought big piles of fruit. We had our dinner and got ready, and off we went about 8pm, complete with provisions and cushions and blankets. Yes! We camped out all night. We were a little way down the steps on a built-up stand, and were able to lie right down and even manage a bit of sleep. It was quite thrilling to lie and look up at the sky and stars – no clouds just then – and listen to the sound of the vast multitude of people as they arrived. It seemed as if all the people in the world were there. The Mall was one seething, packed mass of people moving up and down all the night. They closed the barriers to our steps about 1.30pm, and only the 'residents' could then go in and out. We had a lovely view of the Mall, and through one of the Arches we could see the Abbey in the background.

Everybody got up about 4am, which was also the time when it began to rain. Doris and I sat under our huge brown blanket, which, although it got soaked during the day, really kept us warm and dry. It was jolly cold, and when I went to find one of the specially erected 'Ladies' (horrid word), I had to queue for nearly two hours! The wait was enlivened by watching several carloads of peers and their ladies, all in gorgeous robes, ermine and jewels, and holding their coronets on their knees.

Later, we were vastly entertained by watching the affluent taking their places in the stands; about this time the police and troops moved into position – and we had a band immediately at the bottom of our steps. We saw the red bus taking the little boy pages to the Abbey. Then just before things were really due to start, one solitary policeman on an ordinary bike rode down the Mall. You can imagine the cheers he got – and was his face red?

The procession seems to have started somewhat jerkily. Sheila Wilson remembers it stopping dead while a soldier in the front row picked up his hat which had blown away – and the crowd cheerily singing 'Where Did You Get That Hat?' But it was soon well and truly under way. Sheila Wilson goes on:
The multi-coloured uniforms of the colonial troops were magnificent, and how the bayonets gleamed! Coming from Derbyshire, I gave an extra cheer as our own local Duke and Duchess went by in a coach, on their way to Westminster Abbey.

Joyce Brandreth says:
Words cannot describe it. The crowd, who had waited so long, nearly went mad. The colour was simply marvellous – the colonial troops, airmen, soldiers and WAAF, nursing sisters and a whole squad of Wrens. We were hoarse but had to cheer them all – lovely splash of colour when the Beefeaters came and the Lifeguards of the Queen's Watermen all in red. Then the wonderful Canadian Mounties on beautiful horses – all the same dark brown – their coats shining and harness gleaming. It wasn't raining then, but rather dull. Then the carriages started coming. We couldn't see inside them all, but the Queen of Tonga was the only one in an open carriage and she was a wonderful person: smiling and waving and looking up and down at everyone.

Queen Salote continued to wave and smile, even after the rain began. She is one of people's favourite memories of the entire Coronation procession. As Pat Freestone explains:
She had insisted, despite the rain, that she should be in an open coach, and it was wonderful to see her enjoying the occasion so and waving to the crowds with both arms aloft, big, black and jubilant.

Pamela Barnett and Patricia and Peter Elcoate engaged in another favourite pursuit of procession-watchers: picking out the famous. Pamela Barnett writes:
It was great fun 'celebrity spotting'. I have a set of black-and-white 'on-the-spot' photos taken by a fellow LMH (Lady Margaret Hall) student from Japan, to remind me. Queen Salote of Tonga, a very large and regal figure totally dominating her male companion and defying the weather in an open carriage, received a specially warm welcome. We picked out Pandit Nehru by the familiar white headgear, Sir Winston and Lady Churchill, the Gloucesters and Kents, the Queen Mother and Princess Margaret, and then the Queen herself in her fairy-tale coach. I wrote in my diary later: 'When the Queen came, I wanted to cry a bit, it was so wonderful. She looked indescribably beautiful – all diamonds – so delicate and frail.'

Patricia and Peter Elcoate write:
We rattled off many names to one another as cars and coaches went by, punctuating the known with a few 'don't knows' or 'didn't sees'. The briefest glimpse of 'Winnie'; Mountbatten; the wax-like figure of the Duke of Gloucester; Margaret; the Queen Mother. Our field of vision became increasingly restricted as the crowd shifted about, and the steady rain caused more and more people to try and protect themselves.

Finally, the personal escort of Life Guards indicated the arrival of the golden royal coach. The cheers increased as the coach went by, with the Queen looking lovely. The long wait in the soggy day had proved well worth it.

Peggy Close Riedtmann's account (written at the time) goes into more detail:
When things really got going and the various processions began, I really can't find words to tell you how excited we were. It was like something from the *Arabian Nights*. We yelled our heads off for 'dear old Winnie' and his wife: he looked out of his carriage properly, so we saw him clearly. The Princes and Princesses of The Blood Royal we also saw well: they were riding in coaches absolutely dripping with gold braid, tassels, etc. The horses were so proud and looked perfect. I thought that Princess Mary looked nicer than I've seen her, and both young Alexandra and her mother are very attractive. Never having seen the Queen Mother in the flesh before, I was thrilled: she is sweet and lovely, and the crowd showed her it thought so too.

Princess Margaret I only briefly remember, though I saw her quite clearly.

Then came the start of the Queen's procession, and the supreme moment when the golden coach appeared. I shall never forget the gleam of sunshine which came through as the golden coach came down The Mall. There were lovely grey horses, glittering harness and then that unbelievable coach, so gold and so high, so that the Queen and Duke were clearly to be seen.

After the procession had gone, I really felt quite drunk with all the colour and pageantry: the Guards in their red tunics, the Beefeaters in their costumes, the lances and pennants of the escorts, the gold and crimson of the coaches, the glitter of the Queen's and the royal ladies' jewels – oh! it was gorgeous, gorgeous, gorgeous! We were worn out with cheering, and were glad to sit down, and listen to the BBC, who obligingly broadcast everything to us. We followed the service, and it will forever be linked in my mind with the view across the Mall, between the trees and through the filigree of the arches, and over to where the Queen was in the Abbey, so solemnly making her vows. We sang the hymns with the people there, and when the Lord's Prayer was being said I looked round and saw that many, many people's lips were moving silently, as were my own.

16

IN THE ABBEY

All were envious, and said how lucky we were – and so we were.

Captain E. W. Jackson, OBE

In former times, it was essential that the most important people in the country were present at the moment of coronation because it was assumed that if they were there, they agreed to the crowning, and would not later revolt against the new monarch. In modern times, this tradition is hardly relevant. What does remain, however, is the notion that the 'great and the good' are special guests, with places reserved for them in the Abbey to watch the service and the various declarations of loyalty and homage.

In 1953, television allowed the whole nation, indeed the whole world, to eavesdrop on this special event for the first time. But there was still nothing to equal being physically present in the Abbey, shoulder to shoulder with foreign royalty, peers of the realm, representatives of the British parliament, forces, and officers of Church and State. A few 'ordinary' people were also invited, to represent 'the nation'. Captain E.W. Jackson OBE and his wife were two of them. Captain Jackson wrote at the time:

When we heard that we'd been chosen to represent our firm in the Abbey, we were two of the proudest people in England. We left Middlesbrough on 31 May, after I'd been fitted with a new uniform and my wife with a new dress and veil. The train was packed with people travelling to the Coronation. No one but ourselves seemed to be going to the Abbey. All were envious and said how lucky we were – and so we were. On arrival at King's Cross, we drove to our hotel in Lancaster Gate. On Coronation morning, we left the hotel at 5.30am, and arrived at the Abbey half an hour later. Many people were already in their seats, and others kept arriving all the time. The men were in various uniforms: all the services, and those of most other countries too. The ladies' dresses were lovely: all the colours of the rainbow were there. We had a very good view, from seats in the South Gallery, of the procession both coming into and going out of the Abbey.

Charles Heriot arrived at 6.50am. His seat was in the gallery of the north aisle, at right angles to the west door and just beside a pillar – no use for seeing the actual ceremony (though he could hear everything that went on), but a superb vantage point for watching the processions arrive and leave. Even forty years later, his description of the scene (written soon afterwards) brings it glowingly to life:

The first thing that struck me was the narrowness of the building. The gallery opposite us seemed not more than forty feet away, and the steep banked rows of seats – each person's head being below the knees of the person behind – stretched up into the gloom of the roof and gave an accentuated view of the people in them, like objects displayed in a shop window. The aisle was carpeted in blue (the same colour as the upholstery of the grey wood stools), and the fronts of the galleries were hung with blue and gold tapestry of garlands crowned with EIIR enclosing a young oak tree. The candelabra lighting was intensified by rows of arc-lamps along the top of the triforium. These were only switched on when the television or film cameras were working, so that brilliance literally departed as each procession passed from our sight to the screen and the theatre or, on the return journey, to the west door.

Even so, the glittering appearance of the congregation was surprising. By chance, colours seemed to clot together in great swathes – here a crimson huddle of mayors, there a stretch of pale evening frocks dappled by the black of court dress or tails. The whole colour scheme was held together by the ubiquitous scarlet and gold of uniforms. Nothing was still, and the continual slight movement was pointed by an occasional piercing sparkle from a tiara or a bracelet. In contrast, the stonework of the fabric looked the colour of chocolate, fading to a remote ashen grey as one craned to see the fan vaulting.

So we waited, enclosed and almost lulled by the music and the flowing movement. Then, from far away, we heard a pulse beat ever louder on the inner ear, and knew it to be the drums of the bands in the approaching procession – the only sound from outside that penetrated the private world of the Abbey.

A week or so after the Coronation, I went to a dinner of the Engineers' Association my husband belonged to, and the after-dinner speaker entertained us with the account of his attendance in the Abbey. His uniform required a pair of black hose, and he was in a fix because he didn't have any. Then he noticed a cleaning lady wearing a pair, and she loaned them to him. He told us that he put them on still warm from her legs, and the day was saved.

Mary Winstone

When the processions began, they were like a kaleidoscope of colour. Charles Heriot goes on:

I remember the peers and peeresses – the former mostly bald and lacking in dignity, the latter sailing like ships with their long, ermine-edged trains stretched behind them and their thin, bony, English faces reduced to two definite sisterhoods, the old and grey and the younger and brown. There was an indeterminate sparkle of tiaras, except for a few Victorian ones with jewels on springs that quivered and threw an intenser gleam. One had, I think, jade or emerald points: a refreshing colour note. One peeress had a huge heraldic cat of gold with emerald eyes embroidered on her train.

I remember the Comptroller, in his robes of blue and gold over a red and gold uniform, bearing the velvet box containing the Sword and Spurs. Its weight was supported by a broad red ribbon round his shoulders, so that he looked like a celestial hurdygurdyman.

So far as the children of the Chapel Royal Choir were concerned, they looked like angels. (The adults looked like any other church choir.) The Queen's Scholars all wore black knee-breeches with white capes, buckled shoes, and carried mortarboards under their arms; they were all about fifteen, with an air of demure naughtiness. In the procession of rulers and ambassadors, two tiny Orientals tripped along like the Chinese dancers in *The Nutcracker*. The Queen of Tonga wore a red mantle over robes of cinnamon, black and white, and a porcupine quill at the back of her hair with a tuft of flamingo plumes a third of the way up. One foreign princess was wearing champagne-coloured lace and a tiara high and delicate, designed with imagination: exactly what a princess should wear. The foreign representatives were disappointingly too numerous to indentify. Was that pair of spectacles Malan? That odd naval uniform, Malik? That bald skull, Nehru? I'd so much have liked to look into their faces.

But past they went in a burst of Elgar, and all we have to rely on now is photographs.

I nearly forgot Lady Churchill, dazzlingly handsome in her rose-coloured mantle over a silver gown, her white head, held erect, crowned with a most becoming tiara of long icicle points. And Sir Winston, pink and stooping, overborne by his robes and tottering slightly as he walked. Montgomery seemed to be eclipsed by his maroon cloak; Alanbrooke looked far more distinguished.

Prince Philip was the only outstandingly handsome man in the royal processions. His height and blondness, his carriage and his natural dignity made him a figure of real chivalry. Princess Margaret was eclipsed by her mother, whose extraordinary charm – not always visible to the camera – illuminated her already shining presence in its parchment crinoline encrusted with gold and diamanté. The royal trains were held in outstretched hands by the ladies-in-waiting: a gesture that emphasised the heaviness of the material and the fragility of the bearer. The Queen Mother and Princess Royal were the only ladies to acknowledge the curtseys of the congregation – the former only slightly, the latter with a decisive, hieratic nod to right and left.

The Queen, reduced under her robes to an image, apart from us, grave-faced, moving slowly to an unheard rhythm (nobody *marched* up the aisle, and the music was seldom rhythmical enough to cause everyone to walk in step), was genuinely the hub and focus of the tremendous crescendo. Surrounded by her guards and attendants, not proudly alone as the ruler, she passed out of our sight into the theatre at the beginning of the ceremony, returning again when it was over, an even more apart figure (but none the less moving) in violet robes, crowned with the Imperial Crown and bearing the Orb and Sceptre. Her face was pale, her youth and tenderness intensified by the cherishing – I can use only that word – of her supporters. Something unique, infinitely precious and holy, was being slowly, gently shepherded out into the din and frenzy of the crowd outside.

The rest is a blur of images. A Chinaman in peach-coloured lamé trousers and pale green tunic, so heavy with metal thread that they glistened as through water. A lady fainting and her anxious general fanning her with an Order of Service – and doing nothing else! A group of six far-Orientals, three in purple silk with broad lamé stripes and light-pointed turbans to match, and three in identical garments but of a shrill peacock green. The blind men and women who were seated behind pillars in the West Gallery, where no one could see anyway – perhaps the most tactful arrangement in the whole gigantic plan. The legendary figure . . . on the edge of the blue and gold balcony; a face of unknown origin . . . wearing a boat-shaped turban of parrot-red velvet, his silent, slight movements made with the almost pathetic unselfconsciousness of an amiable toad – and with a toad's benevolent jewel-eye. And last and most affecting: Adelaide, in her green-gold finery, looking as if a little Gothic statue had come to life and donned high heels and long, black, worldly gloves.

The general's fainting wife was not the only person causing anxiety as the long day wore on. Eric Norris was one of many attendants there in case of emergency. He writes:
I was keeping an eye on a canon's pregnant wife. I was ready to spring into action, phoning the doctor and allowing him into the canon's house. (I had, months earlier, applied for a job as a lavatory attendant, but had been turned down.)

Luckily there was no emergency, and Eric Norris was able to enjoy the comings and goings, and the little details that kept the ceremony human:
I remember a WVS officer saying to a group already on parade at 5.30am, 'All well! Bright and early!' When the processions arrived, I remember Winston Churchill coming into the Abbey, and his wife helping him into his seat. I remember a Guards officer, off duty, guarding a magnum of champagne on the steps to the clerestory; a Salvation Army officer (presumably selected out of many hundreds); Boy Scouts taking messages; an Indian organist watching the ceremony from the organ-loft. I recall the Duke of Gloucester nearly falling over when he made his Homage to the Queen. When the service was over a policeman asked me to put a young Wolf Cub on my shoulder to see the procession coming out of the Abbey into the pouring rain. Where is that lad now?

Music for the service was provided by a full orchestra, a choir of nearly 400 voices, military trumpeters, and no less than three players, in turn, on the magnificent Abbey organ. Harry Coles was one of the choirmen – an honour he appreciated even more because sixteen years before, as a choirboy, he had taken part in the Coronation of the Queen's father George VI. He describes not just the service itself, but the events leading up to it:
For all those participating in the service, including orchestra and choir, two days were set aside when all were obliged to attend, duly robed. These 'Earl Marshal's rehearsals' (as they were called, after

the Earl Marshal, the Duke of Norfolk, who was 'stage managing' the events) were held during the week before the event. Coronation Day fell on a Tuesday; our choir rehearsal was in the Abbey on the previous Tuesday. When we arrived, we saw for the first time what had been achieved in the construction of seating for all who would be present on the day. The church had been closed to the public for months so that the work could be undertaken, untrammelled by the daily hordes. What hit the eye were the gorgeous splashes of colour, the crimson damask of the throne and the sacrarium, or sanctuary: just resplendent.

The choir consisted of choristers, lay clerks and vicars-choral from Great Britain's cathedrals and university chapels (including Belfast, Dublin and Armagh Cathedrals), and especially invited singers from the Dominions. Naturally the choirs of the Abbey, St Paul's and St George's Windsor were there. Taking precedence over all were the Children of the Chapel Royal in their vivid Tudor costumes – adding not just their voices, but even more colour.

The music was under the direction of Sir William McKie, the Abbey's organist and Master of the Choristers, an Australian appointed in 1941. He was assisted by Sir William H. Harris and Sir John Dykes Bower as sub-conductors. Sir Adrian Boult conducted the special orchestra beforehand and afterwards. During the service, the playing of the organ was shared between Mr W. Harry Gabb, Dr Henry G. Ley, and Dr Osborne H. Peasgood, the Abbey sub-organist.

Preliminary rehearsals for the choristers and gentlemen were held next door to the Abbey at St Margaret's, Westminster. Well beforehand we had been provided with our crimson-covered books of 'The Music with the Form and Order of the Service to be performed at the Coronation of Her Most Excellent Majesty Queen Elizabeth II', sent direct from Novello's, the publishers. There were four rehearsals for the men, seven for the boys, and one was expected to come to the first rehearsal 'note perfect'. Each of us was given a green card, on which eight spaces were marked; a different-coloured stamp was to be placed in each space for the relevant practice, as proof of attendance. We were also given a green, gilt-edged pass, without which, on the day, we would hardly have got in sight of the Abbey.

Up betimes, as Samuel Pepys would have put it, we arrived at the Abbey and showed the pass. Friendly police parted the crowds and we made our way to the South Cloisters, and the Chapter House where we were to robe.

We had to be there pretty early. Several thousand people, all accounted for and expected, had to be out into the church. We had to be seated and ready by 8.30am. We were accommodated in specially built seating, high up. I was in seat 369, just under the first arch beyond the pulpitum and organ, opposite the shining organ pipes on the decani side. (One was either 'decani' or 'cantoris'.) There were 395 of us altogether in the choir.

During the music before the service, there were various processions. The soldiers' muddy boots left marks on that great blue carpet that stretched the entire length of the nave from the West End to the pulpitum. After each procession, however, a team of 'Mrs Mops' appeared from nowhere, sweeping the carpet clean again, top to bottom, in readiness for the next one.

Once we were seated, we had to stay where we were to the end. Nurses were on hand to cater for those who fainted – and several people did. The choristers had been advised, for obvious reasons, not to drink tea or coffee on the morning of the day itself, perhaps a small quantity of milk. All were to be sure to go to one of the toilets provided, before we all formed up in order to process in. We could eat food (just sufficient to go into a cassock pocket) before, but not during, the service. It was amusing from my position so high up, to watch a peer, seated at the front of the north transept, deftly release his arms from his flowing ermine, extricate a napkin full of 'eats' hidden in his coronet, and eat a quick snack from his lap, quite oblivious of the fact that he could be seen from above.

With a great entry of organ, orchestra and trumpeters – the latter all assembled on the pulpitum – the stirring anthem began: 'I was Glad', to Parry's jubilant music. The service had begun! The Parry had become a tradition: this was its fourth Coronation. In it Parry had incorporated the '*Vivats*' shouted by the Queen's Scholars of Westminster School; this was followed by a *tutti*, the trebles on a top A, sung *fortissimo*. During this anthem, Her Majesty was being

A friend of mine who camped outside the Abbey for a week before the great event, told me that when from within the Abbey they heard over the loudspeakers the question addressed to the assembled lords and ladies, 'Do you accept Elizabeth as your Queen?' and the response '*Vivat! Vivat!*', a schoolboy broke ranks and adopting a pugilistic attitude, cried, 'Yes! And I'll take on anyone who dares to say no!'

Daphne Stone

conducted the whole length of the nave. In the score, sixteen bars before the Scholars' salutation '*Vivat Regina! Vivat Regina Elizabetha! Vivat! Vivat! Vivat!*', there begins a rousing march theme for full orchestra and organ. On its very first jubilant chord, timed to the very second, the Queen stepped into the quire from under the pulpitum.

At such an important event, nothing is left to chance. Technicians and electricians hovered around from Harrison & Harrison Ltd, who had built the organ in 1937. What if there were suddenly a fuse, and its blowers failed? Seated where I was, I could see the gleaming metal of the pipes of the Tuba Mirabilis, voiced on extremely high wind pressure. Behind them, in the Solo Organ's 'swell box', lay a battery of others of the same timbre. At the actual moment of crowning: '. . . and the trumpets shall sound, and by a signal given, the great guns of the Tower shall be shot off' – the louvres of the Solo Organ chamber swung wide open, to reveal all its ranks behind, and every pipe just . . . SPAT SOUND. The poor electricians, lined up immediately in front of the pipes, and not expecting this onslaught, covered their ears and genuflected, to a man!

As a musician, Harry Coles has some particularly sharp comments to make about the way the service was reported on radio, television and in the cinema:

Those of us in the Abbey had no idea what was being broadcast simultaneously to the millions throughout the world. But we heard recordings afterwards, and Richard Dimbleby had a field day! At every possible moment, in his impeccable diction and in solemn and sepulchral tones, he explained in detail what was worn, by whom, who stepped where, who did this and who did that. Much of this talk was trivial, and caused the music of the Homage Anthems, in particular, to be but a travesty, 'jammed' by his voice. His commentary, so far as the BBC was concerned, took precedence over everything. More nauseating still was the music (so called) in the two films later released to the cinemas: a few bars of this, a few bars of that, a snippet of the other, utterly infuriating to those who, after so much preparation, had participated. Over this music, too, the commentators hardly ever took a breath. The film industry is a law unto itself, and is not necessarily imbued with sensitivity to the arts.

While all this was going on inside, watched on TV and heard on the radio by millions, outside in the street William Davies BEM and his fellow servicemen (who had been lining the processional route) were taking a well-earned rest:

Our squad was positioned in Whitehall, near the Cenotaph, and during the Abbey service (which was relayed to the crowd) large laundry baskets on wheels came around and gave us meal-bags containing Spam sandwiches, chocolate and barley sugar sweets, which we all gave to the children in the crowds squashed behind us. Before we had time to finish our sandwiches, the baskets reappeared to collect the rubbish.

Once we'd eaten, there came the only break we had. It was called, 'Exercise Heads' (that's toilets) – and at this command every fourth sailor downed his rifle and doubled away to the Admiralty Building, where we were directed to a basement toilet. When he returned, the next man went, and so on until all had 'pumped ship'. Apart from that we had to stand still where we were. It was pouring with rain, and the white blanco on our caps ran down into our faces. People from the St John's Ambulance corps wiped it from our eyes with wads of cotton wool.

William Davies and his colleagues had to be back on duty well before 2.50pm, when the processions began to leave the Abbey. The Abbey itself cleared surprisingly quickly: by 3pm, the last of the dignitaries had left, and the musicians, churchmen and 'ordinary' spectators were free at last to stretch their legs and leave. For many of them, too, the next stage was lunch – as Captain Jackson recalls:
We went straight to Church House for lunch. There we had a glimpse of the most lovely dresses and beautiful fur wraps. Everyone seemed to be ready for the food provided. We then returned to our car and back to the hotel, having had the most wonderful day of our lives, one which we will never forget.

Not everyone was quite so lucky over lunch. Obviously, everything depended on who you were, or how quickly you arrived. Margaret Robinson writes:
I was watching the Coronation on TV, at a friend's flat in Swiss Cottage. In the afternoon, one of our hostess's friends arrived: a lady who'd had an invitation and special seat in the Abbey. She said that she'd had no lunch, because when the doors were opened, revealing a wonderful buffet, the hungry crowd had jostled in and the tables had collapsed. They were all ushered away. So there must have been quite a few hungry lords and ladies that day – unless they were lucky enough to have sandwich pockets in their robes.

17
VIVAT, VIVAT REGINA!

It was all like a wonderful dream.

Peggy Close Riedtmann

Outside the Abbey, and all along the processional route, people had been patiently waiting, listening to the BBC account of the service relayed over loudspeakers. At last their patience was rewarded. Jane Fabb, writing just afterwards, recalls:

Just before 2pm, they came out. Peers and peeresses first, then prime ministers including our darling Winnie who was cheered and waved at, and who gave us the famous 'V' sign. The Duchess of Kent really *looks* like a duchess. There was some delay in the Kents' coach moving off, and the waving stopped for a moment. Annie and I stood up, yelled and waved – and Princess Alexandra waved back. When they'd driven off, the Queen Mother and Princess Margaret came out. The Queen Mother was charming again, but Princess Margaret didn't even smile. At last, after the escorts had ridden by, the Queen, wearing the Imperial State Crown, came out with Philip, still in his Admiral's hat. We yelled! They got into the coach and juggled a bit with the Orb, which she couldn't seem to get hold of. The Queen looked tired and the crown seemed to press her down; she didn't smile and wave as she had on her arrival, but she still looked beautiful. Philip is gorgeous and much broader than I thought. The Coronation coach is like something out of *Cinderella*, but the gold is a bit brassy.

The most unforgettable thing of all? We were waiting at St James' Palace while the crowning ceremony was taking place. It was raining steadily – but behind us a band was playing 'June is busting out all over'.

Mrs V.E. Glazebrook

144

By this time, after a long day in the rain, people had lessened their earlier exuberance, when they cheered for everything and everyone (including dustcarts). Many of the crowd saved their enthusiasm for particular heroes. Sheila Wilson remembers that her section of the crowd gave 'Monty' and Winston Churchill special ovations. Geoffrey Morris remembers 'band after band, regiment after regiment,' and comments that 'to a boy born in Battersea, still wearing its bomb scars,' this part of the procession 'could not be described in enough superlatives'. But for most people, the climax of the whole thing was the departure from the Abbey of the Queen herself. Suzanne Hulott remembers how tiny she looked in the golden coach. But like almost everyone else, Ellen Poole was entranced:

I really only had eyes for her. She was beautiful, her tiara flashed and dazzled, her smile was infectious, she took my breath away. I couldn't cheer, I could only gaze in wonder. I hold that memory in my heart.

I was one of the Wrens lining the route. People kept giving us chocolate which we had no time to eat. We stored it under our caps (as it was not allowed in pockets), then went back to our temporary quarters at Kingston with melted-chocolate hairdos, to see on TV what we'd missed.

Philomena Cooper

Geoffrey Morris and Eileen Fry (then Eileen Cottrell) were school-children watching on the Embankment. They both have the same memory – one which must be shared by thousands of people. Geoffrey Morris says:

When the Queen's coach passed, she looked directly at me as I was screeching myself hoarse.

Eileen Fry puts the same thought in a question:

Was it imagination or had she really seen me? Was she really waving just to me? In that fleeting moment I was sure our eyes had met. Was it possible that she had noticed Eileen Cottrell, aged thirteen, from Form 1110 of The Lady Edridge Grammar School?

As the procession moved along its route, many people braved the crowds and followed it. Peggy Close Riedtmann (in a letter written at the time) says:

By now we were really soaking, and more than a bit chilly. So we walked briskly as far as Oxford Street, which we could not cross; then, by now being well warmed, we stood under our blanket like a couple of degenerate Indian squaws, and watched the procession returning: the service men and women marching, and the Queen looking really radiant with the Imperial Crown, Orb and Sceptre. It was all like a wonderful dream.

After that, it was time to leave. Peggy Close Riedtmann goes on:
You can imagine that by the time Doris and I got home, we were almost flat out with excitement. We looked awful wrecks: Doris' face had become navy-blue, from being touched by the wet blue gloves, and my hat, which is gathered at the back, was twisted round and stuck out over my left ear. Daphne and Ian burst into shrieks of laughter when they saw us. We had baths and hot drinks, and were able to see the flypast on the TV. We had intended to go and see the lights switched on, but it was too cold and wet, so we stayed in.

Pamela Barnett remembers leaving for home at about 5.30pm, after some thirty-one hours on the pavement, which she says were 'worth every moment'. Pamela Bowen says that everyone round her 'talked for a while', then made their various ways home, 'stepping over numerous sleeping bags, etc., strewn all over the pavements'. Muriel Weaver reluctantly left the patch near Admiralty Arch which had been her damp, uncomfortable 'bedroom' – a place she says she still can't pass without memories surging back of that happy and glorious occasion'.
Margaret Jarrett, like hundreds of others, made a rush for the Palace, but the crowds were too thick and so she reluctantly made for the station and home. She remembers that 'the happy atmosphere continued even in the train, as we exchanged stories of our day with the other people in the carriage'. Pat Freestone says that by the time they were able to fight their way through the crowds, it was about 6pm – and that street-cleaners were already 'clearing papier-mâché pavements'. Doris Matthews and Patricia and Peter Elcoate also remember the after-effects of all that rain. Doris Matthews recalls 'a disconsolate squad of airmen', who'd been on duty since early morning and were now marching to their dismissal point, their uniforms streaked with blanco diluted by the rain. Patricia and Peter Elcoate write:
As the crowd dispersed and we moved off our slightly raised bank, we saw that spectators had created an inch-deep mess of wet

newspaper and other garbage, which completely obscured the grass. So much for all those *Daily Mirror* rain hats. It seemed appropriate to take a walk down to Buckingham Palace, and then to see how the ducks in St James' Park had fared. (They'd probably had their fill of wet sandwiches.) Then we headed for the river, and back towards Charing Cross Underground. We'd no idea what time it was by then, but as we walked to the Embankment it seemed as though the crowds were worsening, and, as we headed towards the station, we had a moment of panic in a back street as the pressure of people became almost unbearable. An ambulance had temporarily stopped trying to force its way through – the story went about that it contained an expectant mother on her way to hospital.

By the time some people got home, they were absolutely exhausted – like Audrey Berry and her husband, who had been invited to a party, but 'were soaked to the skin, hungry and tired, so we just had a hot bath and fell into bed'. Others rushed to watch the whole thing again on television. Jane Fabb was particularly delighted to see the service from the Abbey, and the fireworks display: the first repeated on film, the second shown live as it happened. Ellen Poole, the schoolgirl from the Embankment, remembers the commentator saying that when the Queen and Duke were shown going past the Embankment, the cheering came well after the couple had passed by. She said, 'That's true. We were really lost for breath. We just stood in awe, then came to life as they passed and cheered like billyoh.' Phoebe Ames watched the RAF flypast on TV, then went to bed and slept 'for ten hours without waking'. She adds 'I never regret the thirty hours I spent watching the Coronation, but I wouldn't want to do it now!'

For other people, there were still plenty to do. Geoffrey W. Shardlow, a serving soldier, had had a day's leave to watch the procession. But there was more to come. He writes:
My friend, a staff car driver, was to take his air marshal to the banquet at Buckingham Palace that evening. He, the driver, requested and it was agreed – a rare event, precipitated by the Coronation, no doubt – that I travel in the front seat with him. We proceeded to Buckingham Palace, through the gates, under the archway and into the courtyard. The courtyard was lit up, busy and full of dignitaries in their evening clothes and regalia. Another first – a visit to Buckingham Palace on Coronation night. Would this day never end? No. After parking the car, we went to see the giant firework display in Hyde Park – and bear in mind, in the 1950s a

display of fireworks was a rarity. We finally got to bed, after thirty hours non-stop, in the early hours.

Molly Hames was among those lucky enough to find places in the Mall ('packed like sardines') to see the Royal Family make its appearances on the Buckingham Palace balcony. Afterwards, she remembers:
. . . we walked about looking at the beautifully decorated hotels and shops. We tried to book into a few hotels for the night, hoping to get dry and have a meal that was not soggy. But of course everywhere was booked up, so once more we went down the Mall. Princess Mary's car swept past, nearly knocking us over. She looked wonderful: her skin was flawless and she was smiling. As a child I'd once presented a purse to her and thought her very grumpy. We saw the Queen and her family appear for the last time on the balcony, to deafening cheers. We made our way to the Embankment and watched the fireworks display and then went to see the spectacular street-lighting displays. Then tired, happy and still very damp, we made our way back to the car. Somewhere on a common on the way home we stopped to sleep for a few hours; we arrived home about 10am next morning.

Sheila Wilson also remembers the Royal Family appearing on the balcony:
We watched the RAF flypast from Oxford Street, then made our way to Buckingham Palace where we saw the small Prince Charles and Princess Anne in an upstairs bedroom window at around 7pm. We waved to them for five minutes. The Queen and Prince Philip appeared on the balcony for about five minutes at around 7.25pm. After cheering them, we left and went down the Mall to Trafalgar Square, where troops were dancing. We went on to Piccadilly Circus and back to the Mall, where we listened to the Queen's speech. Then we returned to Buckingham Palace at 9.45pm. The balcony was illuminated. The Queen and party came on to it again, and the Queen switched on the lights in the Mall. When the Royal party went inside, the Palace was floodlit. It was breathtaking.

By contrast with Londoners who braved the crowds, people in country towns often had a much less sardine-like time – at least to begin with. David Dixon writes:
My parents, brothers and I spent the day watching the Coronation on TV at the Lloyds' home, despite the fact that my virtually teetotal and chapel-going father had little in common with Mr Lloyd, a jovial

giant much given to popping out to the pub of an evening. But later on Arthur and I roamed the streets: part of a massive number of people killing time before the events on the Market Square (a talent competition and a fireworks display). It seemed that everyone in the county was in town that day; we were lucky not to get crushed.

The talent contest proved surprisingly popular. The small, canvas-topped stage played host to singers, Shakespearean recitations, and the hit of the night, Mrs Tachi of the local plant nursery, doing a one-woman song-and-dance act totally in mime. After her the fireworks was almost an anticlimax.

In addition to this large gathering, there were many children's street parties, held in our case on one of the larger greens in the centre of our estate. At this, a conjuror amazed me by chewing razor blades and producing them from his mouth strung on a long thin thread. But on a day when news had come of Everest being conquered, on a day when the Queen had been crowned, it seemed as if anything at all was possible.

After a hard day's work in London, looking after people in the Gaumont Cinema, Haymarket, Marion Bunting spent the evening with her fiancé:
The cinema manager had given me £1 tip for the day's work, and we had a slap-up meal followed by a show at the old 'Met' music hall in the Edgware Road.

Eileen Fry, a young teenager at the time, remembers Coronation Evening for something almost as thrilling as any other of the great day's events:
In the evening I walked to Thornton Heath with my two friends. We watched a great firework display – and what was even more, I actually met a boy there. He was sixteen, almost grown up. He followed us all the way home, and eventually asked for a date.

In Dundee, Irene Dowie went to a Coronation Ball. She remembers that it was so cold that she wore her fur coat – and also that the ball was given in the auditorium of Caird Hall, which was usually used for orchestral concerts. The floor of the auditorium sloped, which made the ball particularly interesting. Peter Simmonds, after a hard day's work looking after guests at his firm's London office, went to relax by watching a free performance of a Shakespeare play in Regent's Park. Unfortunately, he says:

. . . I don't remember much about the play: I was so tired that I must admit to falling asleep during the performance.

But Jane Fabb has the last word. The end to her day, and her reaction to being present, personally, at the whole event, are typical of most of the people who wrote to us:

When it was all over we went home. We were lucky, getting trains and buses very quickly: in fact we arrived at Annie's house before the Queen and her procession got back to the Palace. Our parents were still watching it on TV. We joined them to see the end of the procession, and later the appearance on the balcony. In the evening, we saw the Coronation service for the first time, and then the fireworks.

It was a SUPER day. I shall be about 80 by the next Coronation. I wonder if I'll see that?

18

'LOOKING IN'

'Richard Dimbleby unwell. Coronation postponed.'
Caption to an *Evening Standard* cartoon

Except during the war, there had been television broadcasts in Britain since the mid-1930s. At first they had reached only a few tens of thousands of people in London, but the 1953 Coronation boosted the building of transmitters and the sale of sets until TV was available nationwide. All sets were black and white, and most were the size of sideboards or cocktail cabinets; the picture by contrast, was no bigger than a dinner-plate.

Although there had been outside broadcasts before, the Coronation was planned as the biggest ever made till then, anywhere in the world. There were to be cameras outside Buckingham Palace, all along the route, and – another first – inside the Abbey, relaying the service. New, high-speed (for those days) editing techniques were devised, so that the proceedings could be recorded and re-broadcast within hours of the first transmission.

All this was fine for the broadcasters. But for would-be viewers, there was still the problem of owning a set. The average price of a TV set in 1953 was £90, as much as a small car, and about fifteen weeks' average wages. (Today a colour TV can be bought for about one and a half times the average weekly wage.) If you were skilled enough, you could build your own from a kit, as Joan Poole remembers: 'a home-constructed television with a green tube', converted from an 'ex-Government-surplus radar indicator unit using a VCR 97 tube'. Other people watched 'public' sets, hired for the occasion, or in the windows of radio shops. Rita Beckett writes:

At that time our village didn't have a hall, but a local farmer let us use his granary for village gatherings. You had to climb the granary stairs to get to the long room above, which we used for these occasions. On Coronation Day I remember it was full of rows of chairs, and a TV had been hired – a thing most of us had never seen before.

Barbara Browne remembers how she watched the Coronation from Canada:
Mission was a small, mostly farming, community on the banks of the Fraser River. It was, and still is, called the 'Home of the Big Red Strawberry', and on 1 July (Canada Day, formerly Dominion Day) each year there is a large Strawberry Festival, accompanied by Soapbox Derby races. There was one major street, aptly named Main Street, which ran through town with the usual assortment of stores: Woolworth's 'five and dime', a drugstore and soda shop where all the schoolkids 'hung out', assorted small shops, and of course, the furniture store. In the window was a somewhat newfangled invention called a TV set – and it was on that TV, standing outside the store, on the sidewalk of Main Street, that I and many others watched with awe the Coronation of the Queen. How the problem of the eight-hour time difference was handled I do not know. Perhaps we were into repeats even in those days. At any rate, it was indeed magical.

No one we knew at that time had a TV set. Now we (myself, husband and two young adult children) have two colour TVs, a small black-and-white TV, a computer with its own colour monitor and printer, and we recently sold a second computer. Quite a change from standing on the sidewalk, watching in a store window a 'bunny-bear' aerial TV set with its fuzzy, unpredictable reception!

Back in England, Mrs West viewed the events in similar fashion:
I took my two sons, who were of junior school age, to a shop nearby where there was a TV set in the window. A big crowd soon gathered on the pavement. It was a wonder to us all: London then was like the other side of the world.

Phyllis Webb remembers watching in circumstances even more unusual than those:
I was in Paddington Hospital, London, suffering from acute anaemia. We watched the Coronation on a large screen, and for dinner that day we had roast turkey and all the trimmings, with a glass of cider. I hadn't been married long, so my husband was allowed to spend most of the day with me.

Marie Couldwell adds her memory of the day:
My friends and I were saving up for a holiday, so to pay for it I took a cleaning job a couple of nights a week at 1/9d an hour (just short of 10p). We all had a holiday on Coronation Day, so I decided to use it for my part-time work. The lady of the house gave me a pile of ironing to do, a small TV set and a large gin and tonic. I was in my seventh heaven. Whether it was the romance of the day or the gin and tonic, I wept and wept!

But for nine of out ten people, watching the Coronation on TV meant visiting relatives, friends or neighbours. Alan Baker remembers:
The porter where I worked had bought a television set, and asked if I'd like to watch the Coronation with his family and friends. I needed no second bidding. When I'd finished work for the day, I made my way to the small house in Fulham, and after hurried introductions was ushered into a darkened room which measured no more than nine feet by twelve, and already held fifteen other people. There it was – the miracle of modern science – a nine-inch, black-and-white picture which was to have me transfixed for the next eight or nine hours.

> We didn't have television, so I booked seats (5/- each, 25p) at the News Theatre in Station Street, Birmingham. The usual price was 1/3 (6d), so this was special and included coffee. It was the serving of the coffee which particularly impressed me. The usherette crept down the aisle and passed it along, in the dark of course – and to reduce the noise the coffee and biscuits were served in china cups but with plastic saucers. Plastic was in its early days then. I thought this an excellent idea.
>
> Margaret Mackie

Stella McLeish followed the Coronation on an neighbour's television:
We all went round to Mrs Clarke's early in the morning: she was the only person locally who had TV. We all took something for refreshment, and I remember that Mrs Clarke had saved up sugar and made her really delicious apple pies. The room was crammed with neighbours, and there were children everywhere, sprawled on the floor. The children got very restless after a while and soon became bored; we had to keep telling them to shut up. Having never seen TV before, I simply couldn't understand how the event could seem

lifelike on an nine-inch screen. It seemed like a miracle to see the Coronation happening before our very eyes.

Jacky Armstrong remembers being with her grandparents:
. . . who invited relatives, neighbours and friends to watch the event. A jar was put on the table top for 'contributions', next to the lamp (which was on so that we wouldn't be 'radiated', affected by radiation). The long room had every sort of seating that could be found, and we sat in rows looking at the nine-inch TV. I wore a red-and-white spotted dress with a blue bow at the neckline, and blue ribbons in my plaits. My grandmother opened tins of ham and made sandwiches for all the visitors, who seemed to come in shifts. I was so proud of my grandparents' TV aerial, and remember looking at our chimney each day I came home from school, hoping that we, too, had at last 'got a telly'.

For owners of sets, this good-natured 'invasion' of relatives and friends (as one correspondent cheerfully calls it), meant quite spectacular hard work – as Cedric Parcell suggests:
Friends and relatives, some invited and some not, descended on us, and Beryl was so busy making coffee and sandwiches that she hardly had time to watch the TV. In those early days, people fixed their eyes avidly to the screen, and resented any interruption to their viewing.

Things could be even more hectic if you were trying to watch the show yourself as well as work, or if you had other things on your mind. Harold Mack recalls:
Coronation Day was a national holiday, so I was home from work. Our ten-inch TV set was in good shape, and I had installed an indoor aerial in an upstairs bedroom to receive the signal from Crystal Palace, about ten miles away. (I believe that in those days, if you were not within fifteen miles of the TV broadcast signal, you were out of luck.) Because we were among the first TV owners in the street of council houses, our front room soon filled with neighbours and their children. I hardly saw anything except the actual crowning: I was rushing in and out, using this precious home-time to do jobs around the house, and making pots of tea for our guests. (I make a point of saying 'precious home-time', as Harland and Wolff, the shipyard for which I worked, was extremely busy and I was working seven days a week and evenings, overtime.) Wyn was looking after

the three children, aged seven, five and three weeks – no mean feat when trying to watch TV with a roomful of people.

For Gina Murphy, things were also hectic:
Coronation Day was my son's third birthday, and two weeks away from my daughter's birth. One week previously, we'd moved into the house we'd just bought, and we were one of the few families in the road who had televisions. Our next-door neighbours were elderly, and we invited them in. Complete strangers stood outside, gazing in over our low front-garden wall, watching me entertaining two little boys from the road to my son's birthday tea, all with our eyes glued to TV watching the Coronation. Earlier that same day, still with one eye on TV, I'd not only prepared the birthday tea, but also laid the stair-carpet and hall-carpet. A happy, if exhausting, memory.

Olive Butcher remembers watching TV from the 'comfort' of home:
We lived in a street of old, double-fronted houses, and they had all been badly shaken in wartime air-raids. They also had no dampcourses. All the houses along that street had scaffolding up, because workmen were taking the whole fronts of the houses out. They'd started that very week. On Coronation Day we had heavy tarpaulins down the fronts of the houses. In our bedroom we had a heap of sand; in mother's bedroom we had a heap of cement. All our friends and relations got together with bits of their rations and fruit, and I made a Coronation cake and iced it. (At that time you could get nice little toy coaches: I bought one of those; there seemed to be a lot around at the time. Lesneys, who manufactured them, must have made a fortune.) My Dad had just retired in 1952, so he bought our first TV, and in the evening we had seventeen people, sitting behind those tarpaulins on bare boards on the floor, having a whale of a time watching the splendour in the squalor.

But not everyone managed to watch TV as originally planned, as Pat Warnes describes:
Coronation Day started, as most days did, with being woken up when our two children, both under two, climbed into bed with us. We had a couple of rooms in a large Victorian house in North London which belonged to my parents. When we were suitably awake, it dawned on us that this was a special day. My parents had a

small TV, and various neighbours were coming in to view the Coronation.

My aunt and uncle were coming up from Southend for the great occasion. Their daughter had married a Persian lad whom she'd met at university, and they'd been living in Abadan and working for the Anglo-Iranian Oil Company. There were great troubles within the oil business then (I can't remember the details), and it was unsafe for British people to be in Iran. They had a small son, and so they'd decided to come back to England. They'd had to hide aboard a ship, and no one knew any details about where they were and when they'd arrive home. This was why my aunt and uncle had come to us for Coronation Day: to be on hand in London in case of news.

After we'd got the children dressed and fed, the viewers started arriving. I don't know how we all managed to fit round the screen. During the Coronation service, the phone rang, and it was my cousin and her husband at Liverpool Street Station, just arrived on the boat train from the docks. We piled into my Dad's little Ford Eight to go to the station. We saw no more of the Coronation that day. But a couple of days later we managed to get a baby-sitter and watched the whole thing at the cinema – much more comfortable than squatting on the floor peering at a nine-inch screen.

For some TV watchers, the experience of seeing television was almost as wonderful as anything that was being shown. Others were drawn into the spectacle, absolutely wide-eyed at the meaningfulness and strangeness both of the whole day and of what they were seeing. Diane A. Noble (then a small girl) remembers:
We walked the two miles or so to Aunty Dolly's house. We carried a trifle, which my mother had made as our contribution to the communal lunchtime meal. The meal would be mounds of sandwiches, some of them ham, followed no doubt by tinned fruit as well as my mother's trifle. She'd taken a lot of trouble, even buying chocolate strands and using them to write EIIR on top of the tinned cream. I was amazed at such extravagance.

That morning the papers had carried front-page photographs of Hillary photographed by Tenzing on top of Everest. What a great achievement! Hillary had stood on top of the world, lost, we had no doubt, in wonder at the vastness of it all. By contrast, about ten of us were crowded into Aunty Dolly's little living room, in front of a tiny black-and-white picture.

I can still remember the thrill of hearing the opening bars of

Handel's anthem 'Zadok the Priest', and the men and boys shouting out, '*Vivat! Vivat Regina!*' It was surprising to see Prince Philip swear allegiance to a Queen who was really his wife, and to see her wearing, for one part of the ceremony, a simple white, pleated dress, after all the splendour of the Coronation gown. As a child I couldn't help wondering why the two elderly archbishops anointed her with oil. Since then I have realised that this part of the service is based on Biblical tradition.

After our break for food, there was yet more to see. It was a cool June day and in London – though not in Walsall – the rain poured down. But Queen Salote of Tonga sat calmly smiling, her carriage open so that the crowds could see her. Having already come to terms that day with words like 'periscope', 'bunting' and 'Sherpa', I now heard for the first time of the existence of places like Tonga, saw soldiers from Fiji in skirts, and the brave Gurkhas who had fought on our side in the war.

I had never understood beforehand why there was nearly a year and a half between the death of the King and the Coronation. Now the occasion was so splendid, the ceremony so long and the people in the procession so numerous, that it was surprising it had not taken longer to prepare. I was amazed that so many men and women from all over the world should be in London on that day.

I can't remember any sense of gaiety or celebration as we watched: more a deep feeling of the importance of the occasion, of things happening that had their origins way back in history.

Other people remember the TV broadcast less for what it offered them personally, as for the effect it had on seemingly everyone else around. Brian Garner writes:
Mum was most disappointed that I wasn't on duty on Coronation Day. She'd wanted to look for me on the telly. I was a serving soldier and she'd suggested I volunteer for Coronation duty, to line the London route. But I'd declined, and had a forty-eight-hour pass instead.

Travelling from my unit at Foston (Derby), I couldn't believe the fuss in the streets, when I arrived at Euston Station. Side-streets had bunting and flags draped across, most houses had photos of Liz and Philip in their windows, the family pets were decorated in Union Jacks, and most of the milkman's, coalman's, baker's, greengrocer's horses and carts were smothered in red, white and blue. Most London shops were one mass of flags. The entire female population appeared to be positioned in front of the goggle-box. Most people had no TVs of their own, but congregated at friends' and neighbours' houses.

> Watching the Coronation in black and white, you really got the glitter of the jewels. In colour films, that glitter was lost.
> Coombes Croft Library Local History Group

On Coronation morning, my mother and a roomful of friends took up their position in front of our specially purchased ten-inch Bush TV, with sandwiches and flasks off tea. We males were instructed to 'keep out' all day. My special task was to purchase daily papers – four of every one – and not fold them on the way home. (From memory, I purchased over forty, and together they cost under £1.)

On Coronation Evening, the pubs were open until midnight. I had £1 in my pocket, and visited eighteen different pubs, drinking a bottled light ale in each. Then I bought fish and chips and ate them on my way home – and I still had 5d (2p) change. The same eighteen light ales, at the same eighteen pubs, would tonight cost me £15; fish and chips at the same shop would cost over £2.50.

For children Coronation Day was often memorable not because of the TV show itself, but for the other things which happened round it. Colin Stephens writes:
The 2 June 1953 was the day of my sixth birthday. We lived in Hemel Hampstead, so did not travel into London to see the events as they happened, but went to watch it on TV at the house of my father's aunt, some thirteen to fourteen miles away. My memories include travelling on the local bus to somewhere between Tring and Aylesbury, then taking the two-mile footpath across fields, during a hail storm, to my great-aunt's house where the entire family gathered round to watch the spectacle. As I was only six years old, my interest in the actual Coronation was limited. There were far more important things to be done and places explored in my great-aunt's garden. I only realised that an important event had taken place a few years afterwards, when my mother explained where the 'Coronation sweet dish' had come from. To think I'd actually eaten icecream out of it!

Wendy Smith adds her memories:
We all crammed into the lounge on chairs, sofas, pouffes and cushions. Baby cousin Adrienne was in a pink plastic carrycot on the

floor. She crawled away when no one was looking, and was found, after a panic, under the piano stool. My brother and cousin Paul, aged five, disappeared into a bedroom where they demolished my parents' eiderdown – feathers everywhere.

The Coronation ceremony, accompanied by Richard Dimbleby's sombre voice, was interesting in parts, but we teenagers soon excused ourselves and played Monopoly in the kitchen. My sister and I generally quarrelled very readily, but that day was special and we tried to behave ourselves. We set the table for tea, which consisted of sandwiches, salad, bread and jam, and best of all cake with red, white and blue icing. (No one was allowed to eat the blue icing because Mum had used ink to create the colour.) Dad and uncles drank alcohol, and the rest of us had cups of tea.

Towards the end of the meal, the pony escaped. We caught it, fed the pigs, the dog and the turkeys, collected eggs, and it was soon time for the relatives to depart. In our bungalow, there was no room for overnight guests, even on Coronation Day.

Another teenager at the time, Peter Ryde, watched the broadcast, and took in unexpected details, in a slightly bemused state – caused not just by what he was seeing, but by the devastating event which began his day: On the morning of Coronation Day, my mother suddenly pitched forward across the breakfast table and lay there gasping for breath, her face the colour of raw pastry, her hair smeared with marmalade and toast crumbs from her plate. I was alarmed and incompetent, but finally succeeded in getting her to bed.

Later, reassured by the doctor, I went as planned to my friend's house six doors down, to watch the day's events on television. David and I and his two brothers sat in a heap on a small sofa, straining forward to peer at the tiny screen. It was enthralling, but not surprisingly my thoughts were rather troubled.

The television was doubly miraculous. Quite apart from the well-documented fact that the Coronation was a landmark in television history, David's father had built this set himself. In appearance and glamour it was like no other. The picture was minute, only eight or nine inches wide, but there was a vast array of wiring and glowing valves entirely filling the cabinet, which was actually an old wardrobe laid on its side. It occupied about half the room.

Three things in particular stand out in my mind. The first is that in some of the general establishing shots inside the Abbey, it proved impossible to keep the lights out of the picture. Because of the primitive technology, their sheer intensity caused them to appear on screen as jet black. The effect was so extraordinary that Richard Dimbleby was obliged to offer an elaborate explanation as part of his running commentary.

Secondly, there was one part of the service, the Anointment I think, which took place out of sight behind a richly embroidered screen, as being for some reason too private for exposure to the public gaze. This bothered me a lot. Religious belief was entirely beyond my experience, and the idea that this particular moment was in some way ineffably sacred was quite meaningless. The only explanation which occurred to my bewildered adolescent imagination was that at this point in the proceedings tradition demanded that the Queen be stripped naked. On mature reflection it seems more likely that it gave her a chance to whip out a Thermos and take a couple of aspirins. However, I am still none the wiser. I found the thought so deeply disturbing that I never mentioned it, and whoever gets to read this page after it leaves my hands will be the first person ever to know about it.

Thirdly, like countless others, I shall never forget the Queen of Tonga, bouncing about in her carriage, vast, bulging and irrepressible. Soaked to the skin by the pouring rain, she refused to put the hoods up, and waved to everyone in sight in a wild frenzy of exuberance and excitement. She was acknowledged at the time to have been the star of the whole show, and her performance remains one of my most abiding memories. Her sheer delight and transparent genuineness went a very long way to redeem the otherwise rather depressing spectacle of pomp and circumstance in sodden disarray.

We had no TV. I was asked by a very nice young man if I would like to be his guest, and see the Coronation at Rediffusion, Castle Boulevard, Nottingham, on a large screen. I did go, with my auntie. Noelle Gordon was also there, and some of the cast from the theatre. How I enjoyed it! I felt like the Queen myself, being looked after by this young man. I later married him, and never regretted it.

Mrs Dorothy Ludlow

The statistics of Coronation TV are astonishing. Some twenty-three million people 'looked in', just under half the population. There were 2,203,345 licensed sets in the country at the time, which means that nine out of ten viewers saw the Coronation on someone else's set.

Experts estimate that some ten million people saw TV that day for the first time ever: it was the birth of television-watching as a main national pastime. Obviously, for some people, the day was quiet, a small family occasion such as TV-watching might be nowadays. But for most the TV show was the central event in a colourful, hugely exciting and day-long celebration, as Pat Miller describes:

My parents, grandmother, aunt, uncle and I were invited to a Coronation Day party in a 'big hoose' in Dennistoun. It was to last all day; that is, from the time television coverage started till almost bedtime. Right away, of course, I've told you that the people in the 'big hoose' had television, which was not common in Glasgow at that time.

Even before the day came there was preparation to be made, and part of that was that my mother knitted me a red waistcoat with white stripes, to be teamed with a navy skirt and a white blouse; red, white and blue. I thought it was terrific. When we arrived there were seats set out in rows in the lounge, with the TV set on a high table so that everyone could see it. There seemed to me then to be a lot of people, and even looking back on it there must have been forty or fifty there – quite a crowd for a house party, but it has to be said she was a very generous woman. We watched the procession to the Abbey, the ceremony itself, and the procession back to the Palace and during all this, because it took quite a time, endless sandwiches and cakes were eaten, countless cups of tea were drunk and many oohs and aahs were expressed over the grandeur of it all.

Once it was finished and the Queen had made the final appearance on the balcony at Buckingham Palace, there was more food provided and consumed and the singing started. My uncle was a great pianist, and he played while several of the guests sang solos or duets; to this

---

I was Children's Officer for the County Borough of Bournemouth. The children in care, especially those in the children's homes, had rarely seen television. Various people very kindly invited the children to spend the day with them so that they could watch the television. Together with some of the staff, I ferried them to and fro in our cars. On the return journey, one little girl in my car said, 'Oh, wasn't it lovely? But what a lot of washing up! If I lived in London, I would help her mother – I would wipe up for her.'

Isobel Mordy

day I can hear and see my aunt singing 'Dream Angus', and indeed I never hear that song without remembering Coronation Day. The singing and recitations went on all evening until it was time to go home. On leaving, everybody was given a Coronation souvenir as a present. My granny was given a little teapot in the shape of a crown made by the Swan Company, and I got a medal with the Queen's head on it which I still have. After the party some of the younger ones went to a fireworks display in Alexandra Park which went on till after midnight. It was a memorable day – even now, after all these years and many other memorable days in between, I still rate it as one of the best days out I've ever had.

19

CELEBRATING

At our street party, I remember one old man had a red,
white and blue knitted 'thing' on his head. We didn't know if
it was a hat or a tea cosy, and he was a funny old codger so
nobody dared ask.

Pat Wilson

*The 20th century saw a boom in new forms of entertainment: radio,
films, television. They all turned people into spectators. You entertained
yourself not by doing things, but by watching or listening to other people.
This was quite different from earlier times, when people used to get
together for entertainment such as feasting, dancing and doing 'turns'.*

*After the war, the government was anxious to keep the feeling which
had helped us win: that we were a united country, working and facing
the world together. They treated the Coronation as the heaven-sent
opportunity for a national knees-up. They sent ideas to every mayor,
vicar and head teacher in Britain – ideas for pageants, carnivals, sports
days and parties of every kind. For months before Coronation Day the
whole country buzzed with excitement: we were all like children looking
forward to a treat.*

*Of course, community events had to be organised. Lottie Ashenden
explains how this was done, after her street decided to hold a party:*
A lady, Peg, became our organiser. She chose some of the women to
help her: I was one, but I forget the names of the others. We
arranged jumble sales, raffles, tea and home-made cakes to raise
funds. We wrote to different companies and they were very generous.
Peg also arranged with someone to allow us to use the soldiers' large
hall if it rained (which it did).

Pat Wilson remembers another way of raising funds:
For weeks before the big day, every house in the street put 3d (just

163

over 1p) in the kitty. This raised enough for us to provide a meal for everybody, plus a present and a balloon for every child. I think we did very well.

Kath Price writes:
We collected tins of fruit, salmon and meat, and people gave jellies, trifles, bottles of lemonade and cash. The local pub lent us trestle tables and stools, and factories gave us bunting in red, white and blue to decorate the street, and we bought every child a paper hat, a balloon and sweets.

Mrs A. Southon remembers preparations for a huge, estate-wide party in Enfield:
Each street planned its own special treat. The whole estate was decorated, windows with pictures of our Queen in her sparkling jewelled crown and beautiful dress, so regal, looking out on everyone enjoying her day. Flags flew high and across the streets.

The day of the party arrived. There was not a cloud in sight. Early in the morning, the menfolk were busy erecting a stage for performers, fixing lights, finding and putting up a loudspeaker so that everyone could hear announcements and proceedings during the day. Failures to get the speaker sounding right started the day off with laughter. People living nearby wondered what was going on, investigated the cause and joined in with offers to decorate the stage, lend a piano, a gramophone for the music – all offers gratefully accepted. Ladies were already setting up tables in Connaught Avenue, for the food to be laid on later.

In many country areas, whole villages gave parties. Rhoda Woodward remembers the preparations in her home village – and goes on to describe the day itself:
All the arrangements were made by the WI (the Women's Institute). I'm not sure how all the food was acquired, but I do remember that local farmers gave hams, home-made butter and buckets of thick cream. The village baker provided the bread, and we all made cakes. The afternoon started with a fancy-dress parade round the village. The 'band' was a wind-up gramophone that some of the lads had updated with speakers from a couple of old radios. This was placed in the back of a pickup (usually used for transporting pigs but cleaned and decorated for the occasion). Some of the very tiny children, including my son, were placed in the pickup with the music when they got tired, as they went round the village several times.

After the parade, the fancy dresses were judged. My little girl had a frilly, red, white and blue dress and a bonnet, and my son had a home-made Grenadier uniform with a black crêpe-paper busby and milk-bottle-top medals. They were both awarded a 5/- piece as prizes. Every child was presented with a bone-china Coronation cup and saucer, and went to a tea of sandwiches, jellies, cakes and lemonade or tea. We planned a children's sports afternoon, but cancelled it because the weather was so wet and cold. In the evening we had two sittings of dinner for the grown-ups, so that everybody could come if they had small children. I remember we dished up plates of ham with salad and diced potatoes tossed in parsley and butter (which was one lady's speciality). We had trifle and cream to follow. There was beer and tea.

Later in the evening there was a dance. People brought records to play on the gramophone. There would be a couple of dances, maybe a waltz and a quickstep, and then a singing game for the children: Nuts in May or Ring-a-Ring-a-Roses. I can't remember how long it went on for. I think we took our two home about eleven, almost asleep on their feet – and there was still plenty of food and beer to finish off. It was a memorable day in spite of the weather.

> Each child was given a silver spoon with a little medal with the Queen's profile and the emblems of thistle, leek, shamrock and rose on the handle. We still use ours daily.
>
> Isobel Mordy

Richard Balfe's day was memorable for another reason: a splendid example of childhood deviousness:
Free icecream was provided by the Mayor for the children. With a sense of planning which has since stood me in good stead, my sister (then aged seven) and I queued up on a number of occasions each time when we got to the front asking for two icecreams so that we could share them with each other. We also spaced ourselves in such a way that one was always roughly half way down the queue when the other one was served. Amazingly, we were not sick.

Jo Brodie, also a small child, was slightly more innocently amused:
I was busily cutting out the Queen Elizabeth paper dolls which I had for years afterwards. On Coronation Morning I'd been given a large book with the Queen and Prince Philip to cut out, and all the crown jewels, capes and dresses to be cut out and wrapped round the

people's bodies with little tabs. The Queen stood about nine inches high. I've asked many people since if they had similar paper dolls, but no one so far remembers them.

Fancy dress was a vital part of many celebrations. Marjorie Miller's seven-year-old son won first prize, dressed as a cowboy and riding his pony Bonny; later, Bonny gave the village children rides. Sylvia Moore's youngest son won first prize as King Farouk of Egypt, her daughter won third prize as a hula-hula girl and her elder son came fourth as a busy mother with 'Woman's Work is Never Done' as his slogan. Ms Kay Wilson, then a small girl, won first prize as a butterfly, in a green satin costume her mother originally made for dancing classes. There were Laurels and Hardys, Cinderellas, Oliver Twists and – a favourite, this – 'Miss Off-the-Ration': girls wearing dresses with sweets pinned all over them. Mrs A. Southon recalls:

The children's costumes all had to be home-made for the competition. Very splendid they looked when lined up for the parade: princes, princesses, knights in armour, shepherdesses, farmers, milkmaids, yeomen, fairies, Little Bo Peep – and one little chimney sweep, my son aged five years. He was reluctant to have his face and legs black, until we told him that he could carry our own sweep's brush and rods, and reminded him how the chimney sweep pushed the brush to emerge from the top of the chimney and asked the children to go outside to make sure it had appeared and their mother's chimney was properly cleaned. When he took all this in, my little lad proudly joined the parade with brush and rods over his shoulder, black face and legs forgotten.

Gillian Bark's costume was one of those suggested in the government's literature – and thousands of children must have worn versions of it up and down the country. Gillian Bark also remembers another costume, an easy winner on Coronation Day – and the irritation it caused:

I was six years old, and someone made me a dress out of red, white and blue crêpe paper. A seaside hat with a sticker on the front saying 'Kiss Me Quick' was transformed by the removal of the sticker and the addition of red, white and blue ribbons, some of which were left hanging loose at the back.

The great day dawned, and we went to the park. As I had no real understanding of what a fancy-dress competition was, I was rather perturbed to find that I was to stand away from my parents, with a huge group of other fancy-dressed children. I protested to my father, but he told me I would enjoy it. It started to rain as it had been an overcast day, and I remember looking at all the umbrellas and people in raincoats and wishing I was dressed in my coat and standing near my family.

The mayor and other judges came to judge us, and a lady (one of the judges) asked me what I was. I think the idea behind the costume was 'Three cheers for the red, white and blue', but I replied, 'A dancer'. The winner was a girl dressed as the Queen in Coronation robes, and I heard mutterings of 'What did you expect?', 'Fixed', and I think I even recollect someone saying they were the mayor's friends.

The winner was placed in a mockup of the royal state coach which was trimmed with ribbons and pushed round the park by some adults – probably the judges. Behind her went a procession of floats, with children on them dressed as past queens of England. I remember our neighbour's daughter was Queen Boadicea.

A Coronation procession, but of a slightly different kind, was also the order of the day in the party Ellen Cooke attended:
We borrowed our greengrocer's open van, and decorated it with lots and lots of paper roses and carnations. Mums made all the little girls nice frilly frocks. We hired an ermine cape and crown, and sat one of our teenagers on the stool on the van, with a little pageboy to hold the crown on a velvet cushion, and two ladies-in-waiting. Following this van we had four nations: girls dressed in red, white and blue for England, green shamrock for Ireland, thistle for Scotland and leeks for Wales. After them came twenty-five smaller children, dressed in the costumes their mums had made, and holding ribbons attached to a maypole. Behind them came anyone else in fancy dress. The whole procession was headed by the town crier, who rang his bell. A volunteer driver drove the van round several streets and all round our square.

After the procession was over, the children sat down to a tea party in the street, and after it out came the piano, and one of our neighbours conducted community singing, and the dancing and singing went on until well into the next morning.

At least Ellen Cooke's party had fine weather. Elsewhere, Coronation Day rain had a perilous effect on costumes – as Rose Whittle recalls:
My daughter Angela, who was to be married in July, had been chosen as 'Street Queen'. Because we didn't have a suitable dress, we borrowed one from one of her fellow-nurses at Dulwich Hospital.

When the rain came, Angela had to gather the children together. We got them into the houses, but all the colour from their crêpe-paper dresses had marked my daughter's borrowed dress. You can imagine our horror, and how desperate we were to get this dress cleaned and returned to the nurse who lent it. However, we managed. My neighbour cleaned it with Tide, a good soap powder of those days.

Wherever the party, and whatever the weather, the main ingredient seems to have been the children's feast. Mrs Southon writes:
The children's excitement bubbled over as they reached the tables and gazed at the mouthwatering amount of sandwiches, small cakes, pies, trifles, jellies, fruit, cool drinks – all made by mums and friends. In the centre of the table was a large, beautifully iced cake commemorating the event, made and given by a chef who lived on the estate. Amidst fun and laughter the food was quickly demolished, and each child was given a slice of the iced cake and a souvenir Coronation mug to take home.

For one little girl, the day was memorable for not just one feast, but two. Lynne Atkinson remembers:
In the evening, Mum had put us to bed when there was a ring at the doorbell. A few minutes later, Mum came up and said that there had been a lady at the door with leftovers from the party: cherryade and icecream. My brother was asleep; and Dad had gone out. The icecream would not keep. We didn't have a fridge in those days, let alone a freezer. We'd have to eat it by ourselves. What a treat! We rarely had icecream or fizzy drinks at home, and to be allowed up for this exciting supper was so special, I can still remember the thrill all these years later.

As well as parties, there were many more formal events. Liverpool Council took the opportunity of the Coronation to improve one, at least, of the city streets. As head girl of the local secondary school, Doreen Knox had a crucial part to play:
The head boy and I were asked to represent the youth of Liverpool at a tree-planting ceremony to mark the Coronation. Fourteen plane trees were to be planted in Utting Avenue, the road next to the school. The old tramlines had been taken up and the trees were to be planted in new grass along the avenue.

All sorts of people, including the Lord Mayor of Liverpool, were among the tree-planters. I was near the end of the fourteen, and it took a long time before it was my turn. The Police Band played and there were 500 people there. Twelve of the trees are still standing.

V. Gray took part in an event of a different kind: a village sports day. As he remembers it, not everything went to plan:

A comprehensive programme of events had been drawn up to ensure that not only children of athletic prowess could take part but also those who found it difficult to partake in the normal type of events. Event followed event until the throwing of the cricket ball. This event had been included for the benefit of anyone who found running or jumping too difficult, and several of the boys had decided they would have a go. One boy in particular, John S., was determined to make a name for himself, and he had, he boasted, been practising for several days.

One by one the competitors threw the ball. I was the competition organiser, and ticked each contestant off on my list. Some balls went a long way, others seemed to stick in the hands of the throwers and not travel any great distance at all.

John's turn came. He was a big, strapping lad, about six feet tall, and it was obvious that everything was in his favour. He took off his jacket, folded it and placed it at my feet, rolled up his sleeves and prepared to give his all. Taking the cricket ball in his hand and swinging his arm to loosen up, he trundled up to the mark and threw. Up, up the ball travelled – and at that moment I glanced down to the far end, where a big crowd of adults and youngsters were gathered to cheer the winner, and realised to my horror that there was a strong possibility that it might end up in the middle of the crowd. I shouted and waved my arms, and everyone moved back with the exception of Mr Alan Maxey, who was kneeling taking pictures of the event. His bald head gleamed as he glued his eye to the camera . . .

The cricket ball seemed to hover in mid-air, as if looking for a possible target. Then it hurtled down and hit Mr Maxey smack on the head. Down he went like the proverbial felled ox. There was a moment's stunned (in more ways than one) silence. Then the inert body stirred, and there was a rousing cheer. My headmaster, who was standing close by me, shouted to John, 'You're the winner, no more competitors', and down we dashed to survey the damage. Fortunately Mr Maxey had recovered, and apart from two beautiful 'shiners' was none the worse for his adventure. John was the hero of the day: there can't be many people in the world who can boast of hitting such a small target at a range of something like 150 yards.

The boy next door was given one of those models of the Coronation coach, complete with horses. But it was too delicate to play with, and was kept in glorious isolation, out of reach on top of the mantelshelf.

Ian Roberts

Another sports event, recalled by Harry Reeve, had an international flavour. It took place in Edmonton, London, and the guests of honour were fifty young people from Switzerland. Staunch republicans, they were somewhat bemused about the cause of all the celebrations, but there's no doubt, from Mr Reeve's account, that the afternoon was fun: Events included a challenge rounders match on the school field, netball, Swiss flag waving and English and Scottish country dancing, plus the usual games and social dancing.

Many schools celebrated the Coronation by mounting pageants. At Mrs C.S. Thornton's secondary school, the theme was Elizabethan England, and the events included a display of Tudor dancing in dresses 'made as authentic as possible', and the construction of a knot garden (a maze-like formal garden, popular in the days of Elizabeth I). At Elwick Junior School's pageant, Jacky Armstrong (then a girl of ten) played the female explorer Gertrude Bell, and her friend Patricia Lee played Elizabeth I, a part for which Mrs Armstrong says she was ideal because of her 'tight, curly ginger hair'. Frederick Walkden's daughter played Britannia at her school pageant – and needed a little bit of parental help: She had to deliver Shakespeare's speech 'This royal throne of kings', and I coached her for this at home. I told her to keep her head up, and not to look at the audience, but to keep her eyes just above the heads on the back row. I also had to provide a golden helmet with a red crest (made from of a chip-basket and crêpe paper), a trident (the prongs of which were cut from an old iron bedstead we found on the shore) and a shield (made from corrugated cardboard covered with a Union Jack).

Bernard Polley and his sister Jeanne gave a puppet show. They made the puppets and costumes themselves, and rehearsed for days. Originally the performance was to be in the front garden, but rain

made them move to Bill Brooks' garage instead – a venue Mr Polley
recalls as 'hot and steamy'. The programme was as follows:
A puppet looking like Jimmy Durante played the piano (we used a
78rpm record of 'The Lost Chord'). A lifelike doll of Winston
Churchill recited one of his famous speeches (again to a record). The
grand finale was the Coronation procession, complete with the Queen
in her coach, to the music of the 'Coronation March'.

Doris Nicholson remembers Coronation celebrations of a unique kind.
She was involved with the Guides, and their 'Coronation tribute'
consisted of doing 'good works' for the community. She says that there
were so many activities, so varied, that it is hard to remember them all
individually, or to guess how many people benefited, and she goes on:
Some Brownies collected coal that had been scattered over gardens
by the floods. Many Guide companies cleaned churches and village
halls. Rangers worked in the gardens of the Deaf and Dumb
Institute. Members of the Trefoil Guild made toys and clothing for
children. All gave thought for other sections of the community and,
by their work, showed that, as a nation, we are all part of one
another. Many looked even further afield, and sent gifts to refugees
in Germany, the Arab states and the leper colonies in Africa. A
fascinating follow-up was that a large number of Guide companies
later said that they'd so enjoyed their chosen form of service that
they continued it after Coronation Year.

The feeling suggested there, that we were all part of a single
community, and should share our work and pleasure, was echoed by
most of the people who wrote to us about their Coronation experiences.
Mrs E.M.G. Rogers says that the day and its celebrations 'left a lovely
feeling of kindness, happiness and good neighbourliness'. 'Su' Bentham
remembers one of a huge chain of bonfires, lit as darkness fell to unite
the country: a way of celebrating royal occasions which had been
traditional since Viking days:
My clearest memory of the day is seeing the bonfire on Ingleborough
Mountain (2373 ft high, part of the Pennine range). For days before,
old tyres, boxes and other waste materials were hauled up manually
or by tractor, then in the evening the fire was lit. It could be seen for
miles.

But Mrs Southon, describing the 'do' which closed the party on her
estate, catches the general mood, and speaks for all who wrote to us:

Everyone gathered together to do a turn on the stage platform: singing, recitation, even card-tricks and ventriloquism. Children, parents and grandparents joined in. When the children finally went to bed, tired and happy, mums and dads stayed dancing, singing, swapping tales, drinking healths until well into the morning. What began with our young Queen's Coronation Day ended with many friends made for life.

20

CORONATION DAY

It seemed as if every other person in Britain was intent on
looking in.

Keith Taylor

*For some people, Coronation Day had other things to offer apart from
the actual Coronation. For Dorothy Royston and her fiancé, it gave
them a precious (and, as things turned out, tragically rare) chance to
spend time together*

I was a newly qualified physiotherapist, and my fiancé (who had been
my friend since schooldays) was a fighter pilot. I lived twelve miles
from Doncaster, and he was stationed near York. We planned to
meet in York for a picnic. I travelled by local bus, then took a train
from Doncaster with my picnic for two. It was raining so hard that
we travelled back to Doncaster together and ate our picnic on the
train. The trains were almost empty because most people were
watching the Coronation on TV.

In Doncaster, we decided to go to the pictures. Normally one had
to queue to get in, but on this day there were very few people in the
cinema. We parted at last at Doncaster bus station, blissfully happy
because the Queen's Coronation had given us a few hours together.

Separation made it a sad Christmas and then unfortunately I was
widowed in January 1954 when my husband's plane crashed.

*Pat Harker also had a welcome day off, and though it was something
of a washout, she made up for it later in the week:*

I was twenty-five years old, and living in Portsmouth. My husband-
to-be was in the Royal Marines, and was on street-lining duty in
front of the Cenotaph in London. I didn't relish going up to London
in the crowds, so my friend and her husband invited me to go with
them for the day to Petersfield, where there was to be an Olde

Englyshe Fayre, complete with traditional ox roast. I didn't really want to see the ox roast, but it *was* a day out.

We took the bus to Petersfield and went for a country walk and a picnic lunch, as the roast was not starting until later in the day. The weather was showery, but it kept bright and sunny for our walk and picnic. I can't remember much about the ox roast, as I wouldn't look too closely, and also we had to catch the bus back to Portsmouth before the roast got fully under way.

We arrived home in the early evening, and my mother suggested that we go to our local park to see the start of a torchlight procession to the Guildhall. This we did, but it started to rain hard so we came home. By this time it was so cold and wet that I remember my mother lighting a fire when we got home – a coal fire, in June!

Later in the week my fiancé was given a day's leave for having been on duty on Coronation Day. So I, too, took a day off work, and we had a lovely day on the Isle of Wight – really hot, glorious sunshine all day.

Mrs B.S. Payne and her husband were holidaying in Cornwall with their three young children (aged three, five and seven). Their day, too, seemed at first to be a spectacular washout:

We decided to motor to Land's End. Soon after we set out it started to rain, but we pressed on. When we arrived at Land's End it was pouring. There we were, all five of us, in a small car. We couldn't see out of the windows because of the rain. We had no newspaper, no radio. I remarked to my husband, 'Today history's being made, our Queen is being crowned, and here we are stuck at Land's End. I'll always remember this day'. And I have.

Fortunately, things got better later:

When we got back to our camp, that evening, there was a huge bonfire and fireworks on the beach, and the children enjoyed it, making up for a damp start.

Looking after young children was a problem for many couples. And even when the children were well behaved, they often turned out to have ideas of their own, quite different from adults', about what made Coronation Day so special. Dorothy A. Jacques of Nottingham remembers:

We were due to come back from Kenya to England at the end of

April, but the day before our flight our daughter went down with measles and we couldn't travel. My sister had been paying weekly for my daughters to go to their street party for the Coronation, and was so upset that they would miss it. We missed it by twelve hours. On the day the Queen was crowned we toasted her health in champagne while flying over the Mediterranean. We arrived in England the next day. I was freezing, waiting in the drizzle for a taxi. All my daughters were interested in – they were six and eight years old – were the goodies my sister had saved them from the party the day before.

For two much older children – teenagers were still called 'children' then – Keith Taylor and his friend Roy, the Coronation was no more than the background to a far more urgent, far more exciting way to spend the day:
I was fifteen years old and Roy fourteen, and we had both been bought brand new sports cycles, the type with dropped handlebars and Sturmey Archer three-speed gears.

I was awakened about 7.00 that morning by Mum coming into the bedroom and fixing something to the windowsill. It was our flag; the Union Jack with a golden spearhead at the end that I remembered had gleamed in the sunlight when it had been used for a similar purpose on VE Day.

After breakfast, Roy cycled round to my house at 8am; the hour at which throughout the past few years we had met on each morning of the school holidays, then walked along the road to the distant fields where we had made dens, played Cowboys and Indians and fashioned bows and arrows from the stems of blackthorn and elder. But this was Coronation Day. The sky was grey, the clouds scudding, the outlook uncertain . . .

Every house had Union Jacks flapping conspicuously from their windows. There was no traffic. We had the road to ourselves. By the time we had reached the built-up areas around Beeston, we had still not seen a single car, and could still ride two abreast. From the roadside cottages, doors closed and hung with bunting and flags, we could hear the commentator's voice on both radio and television. While Roy and I were cycling in a carefree and explorative fashion into the teeth of the rising wind, it seemed as if every other person in Great Britain was intent on looking in when the historic proclamation was made. The buffeting wind hindered us as we topped ridge after ridge, panting, struggling, using arms, legs and lungs until the final downgrade arrived. 'Melbourne Hall and Pool', volunteered the next sign. 'Thank goodness', we murmured.

After spending three or four hours' bird-watching at Melbourne Hall, we retraced our route and remarked on the sun breaking between that metallic build-up of cloud. But it was not till we reached Isley Walton that we saw our first car: a Morris Oxford, if my memory serves me correctly. Then we began to see people: setting up tables for the street parties that were to follow the Coronation . . . Here and there we caught snatches of conversation: 'Did you see it on the television? Wasn't it good? Didn't she look lovely? And Prince Philip – I could go for him myself.'

Roy and I parted company at the end of his road, but only until next evening. When I got home I read the note on the tea-table, left by Mum. She'd gone on to my sister's to watch the Coronation on her television set. Late in the evening my sister's husband would bring her home in the car. Would I like to join them? After eating the meal she'd prepared, I washed my pots, locked the house and set off to my sister's, taking the path along the canal. Suddenly, a bird with a bluish green back and scarlet front flew like a thrown sapphire into the path of light. A kingfisher! My first! I was so elated that I turned and almost ran across the fields to tell my Mum.

Much later, as we were driven home in my bother-in-law's car, and as I went upstairs to bed, I experienced some satisfaction to think that by cycle, car and on foot, I'd covered a distance of just over 45 miles, achieved a small ambition in having visited Melbourne Hall, AND seen my first kingfisher – all on Coronation Day.

R.A. Dowling spent the first half of Coronation Day like many other people in London, but later found other interesting things to do:
Some relations had come down from Manchester to see the procession in London. They arrived at our home on the previous day – travelling by train (none of us had cars then) and we set off for central London, arriving at a position near Trafalgar Square at about 7am. We huddled up in our coats (it was a cold day) and awaited the procession. Eventually we saw it, and everyone thought it had all been worth while. At this point I left my aunt to it, and decided to go to Ilford, where Essex were playing a county cricket match against (I believe) Sussex, and I watched that until late afternoon, when play was interrupted by rain. During this interval, I retired (with others) to the refreshment tent, and I recall actually nodding off to sleep standing by a counter in the tent. It had been a long day, and I was

exhausted by all the travelling, queuing and waiting, all in fairly unpleasant conditions. I have only vague memories of the rest of the day!

Other people were hard at work. Margaret A. Rodgers, none the less, managed to mix business with pleasure:
I lived on a small dairy farm, so my day began in the early morning. My father and a farm-boy did the milking of the twenty-four cows. I was responsible for the dairy work. In those days this was hard, as the milk churns and pails were extremely heavy. Each had to be washed in cold water, then sterilised in a huge oven-like contraption, heated by a wood-burning boiler. After milking, all the animals had to be fed. We had two shire horses to do the farm work, young calves, a big, friendly shorthorn bull, sheep and lambs, two collie sheepdogs, and hens. Once they were all fed, we went back to the farmhouse for our own breakfast: oatmeal porridge made on a black-leaded range. (I had lit the fire and made the porridge before going into the dairy at 6.30am.) We ate the porridge with brown sugar and milk, and followed it with toast made on the coal fire on the end of a long fork, spread with farm butter and golden syrup. We drank tea. Breakfast over, I washed the dishes in water heated by a boiler in the kitchen range. Then I trimmed the candles and filled the paraffin lamps, ready for the coming night: there was no electric light in those days. I made the beds and prepared the vegetables for lunch prompt at 12 o'clock.

After lunch, at 1.30pm, we walked to our village church for a short service, then to the village green where a flowering cherry tree was planted to commemorate the Coronation. Soft rain still falling, off we went to the field where our sports were being held. Great excitement, for mums, dads and children alike. Flat races, a skipping race, an egg-and-spoon race, a sack race, relay races, not to mention the greasy pole and the pillow fight. As soon as the sports were over there was a rush to the village hall for a wonderful meal of sandwiches, cakes, jellies, trifles and lovely hot tea. Suddenly a hush fell on the whole hall. Each child was presented with a Coronation beaker.

When tea was over, we hurried home again. The animals needed their tea, and the evening milking had to be done. While we worked, our thoughts were on the evening activities to come: a fancy-dress parade, followed by an old-time dance again in our village hall. At the dance, someone had brought a battery wireless, and we listened to snatches of the Coronation service in Westminster Abbey.

Midnight came all too soon, goodnights were said and off we went on the long walk home. It was a lovely dry moonlit night, and we could see the Plough, the Bear and the Seven Sisters in the sky.

What a lovely day to remember!

Harry Molyneux-Seel-Unsworth's memories are not so happy. He was serving with the British Navy in Korea, and in May and June 1953 his ship was in Singapore for a refit. Normally, this would have meant a few days' rest for the crew – but not at Coronation time:

For days before Coronation Day, we'd toiled in the sweltering heat to attain a standard equalling, if not bettering, the Army and Air Force turnout. The big day came and a combined force of troops from India, New Zealand, Australia, Hong Kong, the Sudan, Malaya and several other countries of the (then) Commonwealth, turned out for the parade. The weather was stifling and the sweat ran from us like water. Many passed out while on the march, and afterwards we agreed that the whole parade was something to try to forget as soon as possible.

R.J. Allen was a national serviceman, also serving in Korea. He writes:

We were dug in on a hill opposite a Chinese-held hill: 355. To mark the day we were given a half-pint bottle of Aussie beer between two men, and a tank dug in on our hill fired off some red, white and blue smoke. This brought an answering mortar barrage. The tank shut its lid and we in our trenches cursed the gunner for spoiling our brew-up and our card-school.

John Smith's national service had taken him to the Suez Canal zone:

For at least two weeks beforehand, all war-training manoeuvres and strategic guard details (at water filtration plants etc.) were cancelled or reduced, so that the maximum number of troops could prepare themselves for the big day. We spent all our time drilling in the hot desert sun, repainting all the 25lb field guns and practising for a twenty-one-gun salute. If you think of conditions on the fringes of the Sahara, it will be easy to imagine what an onerous task it was to maintain our uniforms and equipment to the standard required. We were not thrilled.

On Coronation Day, with the temperature along the Canal 100°F in the shade, uniforms starched and creased, boots gleaming in the sunlight, with due pomp and ceremony we fired our guns twenty-one times, at precisely (so we were told) the moment of the crowning. As I recall, a strange transformation came over us. We became immensely proud of what we were doing and why we were doing it. No one at home in Britain knew about our salute. In fact, outside of our own regiment, probably no one else knew.

John Smith continues:
On 21 June I was back in England for demobilization. As I was transported from the airport by bus through the streets of London to Woolwich Barracks, I saw all the decorations and flags from the Coronation. Every house, store and street still bore testimony to a rare event, the crowning of a monarch. I know I had a lump in my throat and watery eyes as the significance of what I saw slowly sank in. Then I remembered sweltering in the hot Egyptian sun doing my duty and paying homage to a person and a tradition that made and kept Great Britain the nation it was, and I felt very proud of the small part I'd played.

Sentiments of similar pride must have been shared by Olive Beveridge and her husband. They were travelling to Zanzibar, and took a leading part in a commemorative dinner-party on board the liner Boschfontein, *of the Holland–Africa Line, lying off Aden:*
There were Union Jacks on all the tables. We still have the menu, showing among other dishes *Consommé Prince Philippe* and *Filet de Boeuf Duke of Cornwall.* My husband was asked, as representing the UK, to make the loyal toast, and that was followed by a representative from each nation on board, giving greetings from his country.

H.B. Smith of Victoria, Canada, remembers special celebrations, 6,000 miles from London:
Victoria has always had a holiday to celebrate the birthday of Queen Victoria, after whom the city was named. This normally took place on the nearest Monday to 24 May, but in 1953 the date was changed to coincide with the Coronation. On that occasion, the armed forces, which always led the parade, continued past the dispersal area and marched out to the Douglas Street football field at Beacon Hill Park, where we formed up for a special church parade. At the conclusion of that service, the band of the Royal Canadian Navy played 'God Save The Queen', and gun crews from the Navy fired rounds. The report of each round was timed to reach us at the start of each bar

of the Anthem, despite the fact that the guns were situated on the other side of Beacon Hill and the wind was blowing towards them. The timing was perfect. There were many other celebrations during the day, culminating in a fireworks display.

Mary Winstone was one of many Canadians who listened to the BBC broadcast of the event, despite the eight-hour time difference between Victoria and London:
It happened that my husband was in hospital for minor surgery, so I was alone and went to bed with the radio on. I lay there all night in a kind of suspended animation, listening to the account of the proceedings: I fell asleep, but I could still take in the descriptions of the Queen and the ceremonies. I have no recollection of this comfortable twilight state happening before or since, and was at the time ever so pleased with myself for having achieved it. However, I did fall totally asleep at one point; just when the Queen was going into the vestry to sign the register. I woke up thinking I'd missed maybe quite a lot, but she was just coming out of the Abbey, and my nap didn't matter a bit.

Further up Vancouver Island, Margaret Pollard also listened to the broadcast – but in somewhat different circumstances:
I had emigrated to Canada in December 1952 when I was aged twenty-three. I was a physiotherapy graduate, and had applied for employment advertised by the Canadian Arthritis and Rheumatism Society. In 1953 I'd been posted to a remote community called Port Alberni on the west coast of Vancouver Island, having undergone three months of orientation in Vancouver. I remember Coronation Day quite vividly. I was returning to Port Alberni in a seaplane after visiting some patients in a more distant coastal village. This community was accessible only by boat or seaplane. The plane radio crackled away, first with an account of the successful attempt to the summit of Mount Everest by Hillary and Tenzing, and then with reports of the Coronation. It was all very thrilling, and I felt proud of my British background. I can also recollect seeing the first 'live' TV documentary of the Coronation, in rather gaudy colours. This was shown in a local restaurant for the benefit of the diners.

Phyllis Reeve, from Montreal, also listened to the radio – and, as she puts it, 'participated fully in the general euphoria of the occasion'. She goes on:

I spent the whole day by the radio. My mind was so crammed with images supplied by magazines, newspapers and souvenir books, that I was quite happy with the broadcasters' vivid descriptions. I was at the height of a chronic royalist syndrome which began with the Royal Wedding and has never quite dissipated. I filled six large scrapbooks with Coronation items.

It was possible to watch TV coverage by standing outside shop windows, and my brother, who was twelve, recalls doing this as part of an enthusiastic crowd. He was/is a collector of toy soldiers, and his major gift for that year was a miniature of the gilded royal coach with appropriate horses and footmen.

The Coronation was celebrated not just as far from Britain as Western Canada, but in places equally – or even more – remote from London. Mrs Haydée A. Kent recalls:
My husband was Superintendent (administrator) of a coffee plantation 3,000 feet up in the jungle, called Pampa Whalley. To get to the plantation from Lima, the capital of Peru, we had to climb to 16,000 feet as the plantation was on this side of the Andes. One could get halfway there by rail, to the mining centre of Oroya (where we were stationed for a while). The rest of the way had to be by car, through very winding mountain roads, so narrow at that time that traffic went up or down on alternate days, as there was no room to pass. During the railway journey you went through 64 tunnels, the last one the longest I believe in the world, and with a decided curve to it at one end.

At the time of the Coronation we had Colonel Gascoigne and his wife staying with us. He was a director of the British Central Railway of Peru, the company which owned the plantation. To celebrate the Coronation, I gave a cocktail party for the senior employees of the plantation. As they were all of Peruvian Indian or half-Indian and Spanish descent, I am sure that many of them did not know what was going on. But everyone was willing to have a drink or two.

Phyllis Smith and her husband (who was then serving in the army) celebrated in the Sudan:
Our children, who were then eight and six, were given a marvellous day of entertainment and celebration at our army depot which was quite a few miles out of Khartoum at a place called Gordonstree – nothing but desert except for the depot buildings and offices and a mess. The officers and soldiers laid on races, competitions, lucky dips

and donkey rides, which were very popular. In the heat of the afternoon we had film shows in the mess and a wonderful tea with a special Coronation cake, crackers and balloons. After dark we were treated to a super firework display and a huge bonfire – much to the bewilderment of the (hand-size) desert spiders. All this was followed by a barbecue and dancing on a portable dance floor made in the depot and laid out on the sand.

Back in England, many people had special reasons, apart from the Coronation, for remembering 2 June 1953. Some were not too cheerful. Molly Schuessele's day, for example, ended on a truly sad note:
I had a nice black cat whom I'd called Charles because he was born on 14 November 1948, the same day as the Prince of Wales. On Coronation Day, when the little prince, who was only four years seven months old, was shown to us all, behaving so beautifully in the Abbey and on the balcony of the Palace, my little black Charlie was run over and killed – a truly royal cat, never to be forgotten.

There was also, it must not be forgotten, a whole group of British citizens for whom Coronation Day was not a cause for celebration at all. J.A. Grimes speaks for them all:
It was the most miserable day that I'd spent since those during the war. The weather made it impossible to go anywhere, and there were no entertainments all day. In fact, there was nothing to get away from the pageantry, and outmoded ceremony, of sticking a crown on someone's head who had not been elected, merely proclaimed, a 'ruler'.

But Mr Grimes is not typical of the people who wrote to us. For most of them. Coronation Day was truly special – even if, for some, the reasons had little to do with the Queen. Mavis Abraham writes:
I awoke at 2am with labour pains. At 7.30am I went in a taxi to Highfield Hospital. At twelve o'clock, lunch time, I called the nurse as the pains had got worse. She said, 'Not yet', then went back to the ward to watch the crowning with the rest of the nurses and the patients. She came back to tell me what I had missed. The baby, Anne Elizabeth, was born at 1pm. I wanted to go into the ward to watch the procession, but was told to rest. We had a special tea: ham salad, fruit and cream. At 7pm my husband visited, and told me that they'd climbed Everest. I said I felt as if I had climbed Everest too. No sympathy.

Joan Cutner (from the other side of the screens, as it were) describes an equally busy hospital day:
I worked at St Mary's Hospital, Paddington. I was a diet cook, but the dietetic department was only a table in the large basement kitchens.

The patisserie chef was very talented, and on special occasions would decorate fantastic cakes. On Coronation Day, he decorated a cake for each ward in the form of a crown with gold and silver 'jewels'. I'd always been interested in cake decoration, and he'd taught me a lot in what spare time he had. He suggested that I decorate a cake for the children's ward, in the form of a castle, and with his help I made a cake with towers, battlements, drawbridge and flags flying. The children loved it.

On Coronation Day, all the patients and staff had a banquet that included roast turkey and all the trimmings, and special dishes named after the day. All the wards and the staff canteen had specially printed menus for the occasion. Also on the day, every ward and outpatients were presented with TV sets – a luxury in 1953. Unfortunately, there was none in the kitchen, so my only chance of seeing what was going on was when I took the diet meals up to the wards. I'm afraid that going round the wards took rather longer than usual that day. Everyone was in a holiday mood, and ward parties were held at the end of the day.

Two other hospital workers, both nurses, remember the hard work of Coronation Day. Eve Lecomber recalls a hectic early-morning scamper:
I was nineteen years old and a second-year student nurse. I worked on the men's medical ward of a small hospital near Shoreditch. The sister and nurses made sure all the chores and nursing care were finished as far as possible by 10am, so that the rest of the day could be free for us to enjoy seeing the Coronation with the patients.

And Mary Underhay puts the whole day, and its excitements, into a completely different perspective:
I was twenty-three and a student nurse. Though I lived in a London suburb, I didn't see the Coronation. I was too busy sleeping between twelve-hour night shifts in a busy general hospital.

But the last word remains with two people who had double reason to celebrate 2 June 1952. For Irene Watson, it was as if the Coronation celebrations had been arranged as icing on the cake of a special celebration of her own: her thirty-ninth birthday:

I worked at a cinema. There were four cleaners, the manager and I – and we had a very enjoyable morning celebrating. In the afternoon we went to the races, and although it poured with rain we enjoyed it. I backed a 12–1 winner. We had to get back to open the cinema for the evening's show. I had a birthday cake made like a crown, and a bottle of Moët et Chandon champagne.

On the same day, Patricia Thomas was nine years old – and even today, as she says, 'despite being a middle-aged mother of three', she can still remember the double excitement of Coronation Day:

My younger sister Diane and I got up early that morning. People had been looking forward to the great day for weeks and preparing street parties. Also the streets were decorated with flags and bunting and pictures of the Royals were displayed in people's windows.

After I'd opened my presents and cards, my mother helped us to dress in our matching sun-dresses in red, white and blue which she'd made for the occasion. Then we all went round to my aunt's and uncle's house. They lived a few streets away and were the proud possessors of a TV set. We watched the service and the processions, and then went back to our street in Grangetown, Cardiff, which is quite near to the docks area, and enjoyed a noisy street party where everyone provided some food and drink and we children had a wonderful time taking part in races, games and a fancy dress parade.

21
CORONATION POSTSCRIPT

I was intensely royalist in those days. I have an entry in my diary saying, 'Miss Gardner (office manager) will fine me five cents every time I mention the Coronation'.

Sheila McGregor Morgan

Not long after the Coronation, the new Queen and her husband went on tours abroad, visiting places as far apart as Australia and the Caribbean, Rhodesia (as it then was) and the Arctic Circle. In general, the response was rapturous, though in Canada especially, feelings were somewhat mixed. On the one hand, Evelyn Riegert remembers:
They travelled across the whole country by train. They stopped in our town, and our Glee Club went to the station to meet them and sing 'Oh Canada' and 'God Save the Queen'. We were so awestruck that we almost forgot to sing.

Others were less impressed. In Quebec, there were anti-royalist, anti-British mutterings on a large scale, only partially stilled when the Queen charmingly and unexpectedly broke into (cut-glass) French. As Pat Salmon remembers, people with a non-royalist background tended to show politeness rather than fervour:
'I am a Canadian of Irish-American descent, and thus a Roman Catholic. At the time of the royal visit, I was in high school at Saint Ann's Academy, a select convent school run by nuns of Irish or Quebecois descent. They let it be known that we must perhaps love the monarchy, but we certainly didn't need to like them. We were even reminded that the first Queen Elizabeth had pinched Westminster Abbey from the Catholic Church.
On the day of the visit, the nuns paraded us two by two, in immaculate uniforms, up to Yates Street where we waited in perfect order and perfect silence. We each had a small, stiff Union Jack to

wave to the Queen as she passed. We waited and waited, and eventually they came. I looked at the face of the young Queen, who seemed old, being much older then I. She appeared very alone and slightly pained. I wondered how it would be in life to have all these people who thought they knew you, while you in turn could never know them.

After the parade passed we walked back to the convent. We were not expected to return the little Union Jacks. That was a good thing, as my friend (who thirty years later became Provincial Superior) had snapped hers in two and thrown it in the gutter.

Bob Clarke and his friend Art had better things to do than watch parades:
We were junior clerks at the naval dockyards. The pay was very low, and to make extra money we painted houses in the evenings and at weekends.

In honour of the royal visit, the dockyard employees were given an afternoon off, and were encouraged to line the parade route and wave to the royal couple. Art and I had seen the Queen and Prince Philip on their arrival the previous evening. So we decided to use this bonus afternoon to get some more painting finished. The house was located three blocks away from where the royal couple were staying. It was a wooden house, and we were painting it with a black oil stain. As the afternoon wore on, Art accidentally splashed me with this horrible stain. I good-naturedly flicked back at him. This started an all-in stain fight, and we both ended up drenched in it. We sat down exhausted on the lawn.

Art noticed that a crowd had gathered out on the street. Our first reaction was that there'd been an accident, and we went to see. We still had the stain brushes in our hands, but we'd temporarily forgotten what a terrible mess we were. We could see nothing for the crowds. I stepped through an opening between two people, right into the path of the royal car, which had to swerve slightly to miss me. I lurched back, as the startled faces of the Queen and Prince Philip passed by, only a foot or so away.

Back in Britain, Barbara Allman remembers the royal couple's triumphant return to London, sailing up-river in the royal yacht Britannia:
The Thames was jammed solid with boats of every type and class. The Chartered Society of Physiotherapists (of which I was a member)

had booked a fair-sized vessel, and we had a perfect position. We saw the Queen and Prince Philip in casual clothes on board, where they were joined for lunch by the Queen Mother and the young royal children. In the afternoon we saw the Royals, dressed up, get into the royal barge for the short trip to the pier. The river was a continuous blast of hooters, whistles, cheering, yelling, clapping – everything.

There were also tours at home. Maria Wrist writes:
When the Queen and Prince Philip toured the London boroughs, so that everyone could see them, I took the children – by accident. I don't like crowds, and I miscalculated the time. I'd intended to wait till the event had passed before taking the children out. But the procession was delayed, and we ran right into the people waiting by the roadside. The crowds parted to let my children to the front so that they could see better. A cheer went up, but all that was coming was a bewildered little dog running in the middle of the road. Soon the real thing came along, with motorcycle police escort and all the pomp expected of a newly crowned queen. She was in ordinary clothes, though, and had left her crown behind – facts much discussed by the children.

'Coronation fever' lasted for several months after the event – and could take bizarre forms. Elsie Darby remembers:
1953 was the year I was married, and I remember that nearly all my wedding presents had pictures of the Queen and Prince Philip on them. Someone bought me a beautiful lace tablecloth – and when we opened it, right in the middle was the Queen.

As well as writing about what happened or what they were doing at the time, several of our correspondents described their feelings about the meaning of the Coronation. Peter Ryde's summing-up is wide-ranging, dry and personal:
My parents regarded the whole business as a tedious and prolonged interference with their ordered but difficult lives. My mother thought her cousin from Manchester was plumb crazy to spend £25 on a seat in one of the stands – and not even a covered one. My father, naturally reclusive and a man of few words, confined himself to some very uncomplimentary remarks about the Bishop of Bath and Wells, whose piety was not in question but whose huge spectacles and disconcerting appearance made him a less than fortunate choice for one of the more prominent supporting roles – as a glance at contemporary photographs will rapidly confirm.

As a Londoner, born, bred and blitzed, I had vivid memories of VE Day – and night – in which I had felt a genuine sense of participation. I was much struck by the difference between the spontaneous jubilation of 1945 and the carefully pre-arranged and shamelessly exploited jollification-to-order eight years later. Mind you, as a gigantic piece of carefully stage-managed theatricality, the whole event seemed inexhaustibly fascinating. It was the first time I had experienced anything like it. But I was an onlooker, without the slightest sense of personal involvement.

Unlike my parents, I welcomed the break from routine. I didn't object to finding the streets suddenly blocked, or the skyline disfigured for weeks by the huge networks of scaffolding that formed the basis of the stands along the route. Of course, one quickly got fed up with the ubiquitous red, white and blue (so much so that, forty years on, the new British Telecom logo turns my stomach every time I encounter it), but it was fun to see it all happening.

My chief interest was in the sheer organisation and mechanics of staging such an event or, as we should say now, the logistics of it all. I eagerly read everything that was offered in the way of behind-the-scenes information: for example, that as soon as the ceremony was over, the Queen would swap her crown for a special light-weight one, less punishing to the vertebrae during the coach ride; or that her coach was being fitted with special racks for the Orb and Sceptre so that she could appear to be holding them when she wasn't.

There seemed to be a lot of sense in all this. On the other hand, I was deeply shocked by the decision to dress the marching troops in specially made uniforms of a totally non-standard colour (blue, I think) because khaki did not photograph well on colour film. As a budding photographer, I could appreciate the practicality of such a step, but it seemed all wrong to let the photographers influence the actual event. You might as well say: 'Let's crown Princess Margaret instead, she's more photogenic.'

The attitude of Americans to the whole affair was a constant source of amazement. I don't know what astonished me more: the seemingly flippant irreverence which prompted their headline writers to refer to it as the Liz Biz, a style of parlance for which England in the 1950s was far from ready; or the sight, a little later in the year, of a whole busload of American tourists debouching into HMV in Oxford Street, each buying several sets of the newly issued boxed LPs of the Coronation service, and then carrying them back to the bus with a sort of reverential awe that would have befitted the Holy Grail.

Mrs F.E. Hamill catches a mood which 99 per cent of all the people who wrote to us, and the vast majority of the country at the time, seem to have shared:

I think that whether lovers of royalty or not, all were captivated and caught up in this historic act, made more poignant by her youth, seriousness and air of dedication.

LOOKING BACK ON
THE 1950s

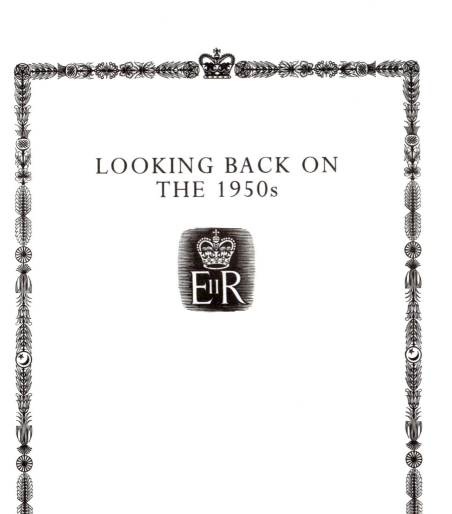

22

WHAT WERE THOSE DAYS *REALLY* LIKE?

My first pair of nylons, which my husband had brought from America or Canada, I put to air on the gas stove. They melted.

Rosemary Ridyard

Most people who wrote to us remember the 1950s and their quality of life then with some affection. Without doubt, the Coronation lifted the spirits of the majority of people and the anticipation, excitement and pleasure of the celebrations gave a much-needed boost, enabling people at last to escape the post-war gloom which had lingered on so long. In their own words, here is a selection of comments on the fifties from people who remembered them. Ronald Coley writes:
It may not have been a better world in the 1950s, but it was most certainly a nicer, more civilised one. When people went visiting, they dressed properly: men and boys wore suits, collars and ties, and girls and women wore smart dresses. There were few who did not take a great pride in dressing up. Appearance was important. Men wore trilbys, double cuffs and links, the ladies hats and gloves. Prams were large and polished – and the babies inside were equally polished, and as well turned out as circumstances permitted.

Maxine Elvey contrasts 'then' and 'now':
It was a prim age. People were formal in their manners. Swearing and shouting in public were far less common than they are today.
  People did not discuss their problems. They kept it all inside. Recently my mother's two biggest problems of the time were discussed on *Woman's Hour* within a few days of each other. The first was that my father was over-conscientious in his work, came home late, and did not see much of his daughters except on Sundays and our annual holiday. The other was that I constantly teased my

younger sister, because I felt that Mum favoured her. Fathers working late, sibling jealousy, and such family problems were never aired on radio in the 1950s. If they had been, Mum would have realised that she was not unique, and probably could have coped better.

Divorce was rare. It was considered a terrible thing, because in those days the main grounds for divorce was adultery which had to be proven – and 'adultery', with all its Biblical connotations, seemed such a terrible word. To get pregnant before marriage was also considered quite terrible.

Children tended to be 'seen and not heard'. Today children participate in adult conversations, their opinions are sometimes asked in family decisions, their voice is heard. In the 1950s this was not the case. In school there were few disobedient children. We just worked quietly, seated in rows. It was also much safer. Mugging was unheard-of, house-burglaries were rare and my sister and I walked two miles to school and back, all through our secondary years, without fear of being molested. I expect that such things did go on, but the dissemination of news was far less sophisticated, so we didn't hear about it, and therefore didn't worry about it.

Many people always retain the 'look' of the age they grew up in, and the Queen in her public persona has the look, manners and primness of the 1950s.

Molly Schuessele reminds us of a smaller (though perhaps no less important) area in which ideas have changed:
Personally I smoked twenty cigarettes, Players preferably, per day. Everyone smoked, with very few exceptions. No social gathering was complete unless cigarettes were handed round.

Brian Garner reflects on security:
All through the early 1950s, the back door of Mum's house would not close – the sill and bottom rail had swollen. This didn't worry Mum in the slightest. Burglaries in the working-class side of East Enfield were absolutely unheard-of. From 1936–52, there had been only one that we were aware of – a chap who ran a loan club had a mysterious break-in just before 'paying-out day'.

For 'Su' Bentham and Peter Wickings, 'simple pleasures' were a keynote of the times. 'Su' Bentham writes:
On reflection, 1953, with its dreams of cars, televisions, washing

machines, central heating and so on, produced one thing in reality: the satisfaction of a simple happiness amongst people who had not been disturbed by such things as greed, envy and wholesale crime.

Peter Wickings adds:
Some people seemed a lot more cheerful and honest than they are today, and we took pleasure in the simple things like the occasional trip to the pictures, queuing for the 'one and nines', or went on family picnics or bike rides into the countryside.

And David Dixon, reflecting on the whole period, sums things up as follows:
In many ways the seven years I lived in Huntingdon during the 1950s symbolised the transition from pre-war Britain to the 'brave new world' of the 1960s. We arrived as the Nickel Coin Restaurant opened its select doors, and we left to the sound of the Fiesta Coffee Bar jukebox. In between we'd seen cars arrive on roads in greater numbers than was ever thought possible, and a huge increase in the lorries that jammed our tiny High Street. As boys we'd seen the last of the great steam engines and propeller-driven aeroplanes. We'd grown up to see 'adolescents' replaced by 'teenagers', and the steady swamping of radio by first BBC TV and after 1955 Commercial TV. We'd seen the end of rationing and the beginning of the 'never-had-it-so-good' years – changes which I saw in the context of a small rural town in East Anglia, but which were happening to a greater or lesser degree all over the country.

I fancy that if I were given a bicycle and a bag of papers, I could still remember the round I began in 1954, for many of the houses still remain. But outside the town, beyond its massive new boundaries, is where the greatest difference lies. The A1, the Great North Road where once we cycled freely as eight-year-olds, is now the A1(M) for most of its southern section – and as I see the names of the villages that used to represent a whole afternoon's effort to reach, piling themselves up one after the other in neat motorway typography, it's impossible not to feel regret at the changes. To travel from St Neots in the south through to Stilton in the north, now takes barely twenty-five minutes. And across the new broad landscape, now largely unhindered by the historic intricacies of hedges, trees and ditches that we knew so well, comes prairie-style farming backed by city companies.

It's commonplace nowadays to claim that the character of English towns and villages has changed more in the past twenty-five years than in the previous 250, and it's seldom that such changes have been for the better. The thought sometimes strikes me that my generation had the best opportunities ever available in Britain simply handed to it on a plate: from free welfare orange juice and ration-book nutrition to further education and jobs for the asking. Back in the 1950s radical thinkers believed that life was lucky for some. Perhaps in retrospect it was lucky for all.